Raspberry Pi By Example

Start building amazing projects with the Raspberry Pi right out of the box

Ashwin Pajankar

Arush Kakkar

PUBLISHING

BIRMINGHAM - MUMBAI

Raspberry Pi By Example

First published: April 2016

Production reference: 1190416

Published by Packt Publishing Ltd.
Livery Place
35 Livery Street
Birmingham B3 2PB, UK.

ISBN 978-1-78528-506-6

www.packtpub.com

Credits

Authors
Ashwin Pajankar
Arush Kakkar

Reviewers
Nathan Johnson
Elliot Kermit-Canfield
Anna Torlen

Commissioning Editor
Dipika Gaonkar

Acquisition Editor
Ashwin Nair

Content Development Editor
Merwyn D'souza

Technical Editors
Nirant Carvalho
Mohit Hassija

Copy Editors
Stuti Srivastava
Madhusudan Uchil

Project Coordinator
Nikhil Nair

Proofreader
Safis Editing

Indexer
Priya Sane

Graphics
Kirk D'Penha

Production Coordinator
Shantanu N. Zagade

Cover Work
Shantanu N. Zagade

About the Authors

Ashwin Pajankar is a software professional and IoT enthusiast with more than 5 years' experience in software design, development, testing, and automation.

He graduated from IIIT Hyderabad, earning an M.Tech in computer science and engineering. He holds multiple professional certifications from Oracle, IBM, Teradata, and ISTQB in development, databases, and testing. He has won several awards in college through outreach initiatives, at work for technical achievements, and community service through corporate social responsibility programs.

He was introduced to Raspberry Pi while organizing a hackathon at his workplace, and he's been hooked on Pi ever since. He writes plenty of code in C, Bash, Python, and Java on his cluster of Pis. He's already authored one book on Raspberry Pi and reviewed three other titles related to Python for Packt Publishing.

His LinkedIn Profile is at `https://in.linkedin.com/in/ashwinpajankar`.

I would like to thank my wife, Kavitha, for motivating me to write this book and share my knowledge with others. I would like to thank my coauthor, Arush Kakkar, for taking over the project after the first few chapters. I also thank Merwyn D'Souza from Packt Publishing for providing me with the opportunity, guidance, and required support in writing this book. Last but not least, I would like to thank all the reviewers who helped me make the book better by providing their precious feedback.

Arush Kakkar is a computer vision and deep learning researcher and an undergraduate at Delhi Technological University. His primary focus is on autonomous robotics, which includes drones and self-driving cars, and he has been involved in building such systems in different capacities, such as navigation, localization, path planning. He has also leveraged state-of-the art computer vision and deep learning technologies for them. He is the electrical systems head of the Solar Car team of his university, Solaris DTU.

He is currently working on his own driverless car company, CruiseX, which uses deep learning to drive more smoothly and with fewer errors.

You can connect with him through his website at `http://www.arushkakkar.com` and read up on some of his projects at `http://blog.arushkakkar.com`.

I would like to thank my parents for supporting me in writing this book. I would like to thank Ashwin for collaborating while writing this book, and I would also like to thank Merwyn from Packt Publishing for coordinating the collaboration. I am thankful to all the reviewers for helping me improve the book and expanding my knowledge.

About the Reviewers

Nathan Johnson is an NC State University graduate and the author and maintainer of the node-arm project. Apart from node-arm, he has also contributed to several other Raspberry Pi projects. He currently works for the Charlotte-based company Red Ventures as a software engineer writing applications in Node.js.

> I would like to thank my mom, dad, and brother for reminding me to use all the talents I've been given.

Elliot Kermit-Canfield is a graduate student studying computer music at the Center for Computer Research in Music and Acoustics at Stanford University. In addition to a degree in music, science, and technology from Stanford, he holds degrees in integrative arts and music theory from Penn State. Elliot is an avid computer musician and has worked with Raspberry Pi and other embeddable systems with audio applications.

Anna Torlen is an artist, educator, and techie. She received a bachelor of arts degree in studio art at The College of Santa Fe and a master of fine arts degree in media, technology, and entertainment at Florida Atlantic University. She has worked on Raspberry Pi projects at her college and at Hacklab in Boynton Beach, FL. She has contributed to the Adafruit Community Corner blog. She is currently working at Palm Beach State College as a multimedia adjunct professor. She is interested in building outdoor solar-powered Internet of Things Raspberry Pi projects.

www.PacktPub.com

eBooks, discount offers, and more

Did you know that Packt offers eBook versions of every book published, with PDF and ePub files available? You can upgrade to the eBook version at www.PacktPub.com and as a print book customer, you are entitled to a discount on the eBook copy. Get in touch with us at customercare@packtpub.com for more details.

At www.PacktPub.com, you can also read a collection of free technical articles, sign up for a range of free newsletters and receive exclusive discounts and offers on Packt books and eBooks.

https://www2.packtpub.com/books/subscription/packtlib

Do you need instant solutions to your IT questions? PacktLib is Packt's online digital book library. Here, you can search, access, and read Packt's entire library of books.

Why subscribe?

- Fully searchable across every book published by Packt
- Copy and paste, print, and bookmark content
- On demand and accessible via a web browser

Table of Contents

Preface

Raspberry Pi is probably one of the most versatile computers ever built. It has been adapted for tasks ranging from home automation, cluster computing, computer vision, and even space missions! What's more is that it enjoys a level of support from the community that is hard to find for any other platform.

Due to this, it is a hacker-friendly device and is a must for anyone who wants to build projects with even a little amount of programming involved. The fact that the basic version of the board costs only $25 means there's a lot of room for experimentation, and users aren't afraid to experiment with and damage it.

In this book, you will find a wide variety of projects, using which anyone can get started with and also build interesting hacks by modifying some of the projects.

What this book covers

Chapter 1, Introduction to Raspberry Pi and Python, provides an introduction to the Raspberry Pi and booting it up.

Chapter 2, Minecraft Pi, introduces you to Minecraft Pi, which is a preinstalled version of the popular game Minecraft. The first few pages of the chapter deal with the game concept and interface, and further pages deal with programming in-game actions with Python. In the last part of this chapter, you are introduced to the PyGame library and small usage examples of it.

Chapter 3, Building Games with PyGame, is an introduction to the PyGame programming library and game programming. In this chapter, you code your way to your first full-fledged program on the Raspberry Pi, a game.

Chapter 4, Working with a Webcam and Pi Camera, introduces you to the Pi Camera and regular webcams and how to use them to create real-life applications with the Raspberry Pi. You also create a time-lapse box project in this chapter.

Chapter 5, Introduction to GPIO Programming, introduces you to the Raspberry Pi B+ and Pi 2 GPIO structure and its real-life usage with LED programming and a third-party add-on, PiGlow.

Chapter 6, Creating Animated Movie with Raspberry Pi, demonstrates the GPIO and camera together by creating a project that requires application of both the concepts in order.

Chapter 7, Introduction to Computer Vision, introduces you to computer vision and image processing with Raspberry Pi. You will create a simple project.

Chapter 8, Creating Your Own Motion Detection and Tracking System, introduces you to advanced concepts in OpenCV, which will be used to implement the next project, which has a higher difficulty level.

Chapter 9, Grove Sensors and the Raspberry Pi, introduces you to the Grove shield and Grove sensors and their interfacing with Raspberry Pi. Grove Sensors are third-party sensors for Raspberry Pi and Arduino that can be used for environment sensing.

Chapter 10, Internet of Things with the Raspberry Pi, looks at creating home automation and Internet of Things applications with the Raspberry Pi.

Chapter 11, Build Your Own Supercomputer with the Raspberry Pi, deals with making clusters of Raspberry Pi 2s, using MPICH2 and MPI for Python to write parallel programs for the clusters, and running N-body simulation.

Chapter 12, Advanced Networking with the Raspberry Pi, shows you how to improve your cluster of Pis by adding advanced networking capabilities such as DNS and DHCP. We use of existing cluster for this and make it better.

Chapter 13, Setting Up a Web Server on the Raspberry Pi, delves into installing PHP, MySQL, and WordPress on our Raspberry Pi to use it as a web server.

Chapter 14, Network Programming in Python with the Pi, teaches you how to use Python to learn the basics of network programming and also create network utilities such as Telnet and chat applications on the Raspberry Pi.

Appendix, Newer Raspberry Pi Models, briefly introduces you to some of the newest members of the Raspberry Pi family, namely the Raspberry Pi Zero and the Raspberry Pi 3.

What you need for this book

The following hardware is recommended for successfully completing the projects outlined in this book:

- Raspberry Pi Model B, B+ or 2 (Multiple boards for last two chapters)
- USB hub, powered preferably
- Networking hub
- PC for preparing SD card
- Webcam and/or Pi Camera

Who this book is for

What's the best way to learn how to use your Raspberry Pi? By example! If you want something exciting to do whilst getting to grips with what your Pi can offer, this is the book for you. With both simple and complex projects, you'll create a wide variety of cool toys and functions with your Raspberry Pi - all with minimal coding experience necessary. You can be a beginner before starting with this book, but by the time you finish it, you will be a Jedi with the Raspberry Pi.

Conventions

In this book, you will find a number of text styles that distinguish between different kinds of information. Here are some examples of these styles and an explanation of their meaning.

Code words in text, database table names, folder names, filenames, file extensions, pathnames, dummy URLs, user input, and Twitter handles are shown as follows: " We need the random library for the randint() function, which returns a random integer in the provided range."

A block of code is set as follows:

```
def fractal_tree(b_len,t):
    if b_len > 5:
        temp=random.randint(1, b_len)
        temp_angle = random.randint(1, 25)
        t.forward(temp)
        t.right(temp_angle)
        fractal_tree(b_len-10,t)
        t.left(2 * temp_angle)
```

```
fractal_tree(b_len-10,t)
t.right(temp_angle)
t.backward(temp)
```

Any command-line input or output is written as follows:

```
pi@raspberrypi ~ $ mkdir book
pi@raspberrypi ~ $ cd book
pi@raspberrypi ~/book $ pwd
/home/pi/book
pi@raspberrypi ~/book $
```

New terms and **important words** are shown in bold. Words that you see on the screen, for example, in menus or dialog boxes, appear in the text like this: " Check out the **Product** page of Raspberry Pi at http://www.raspberrypi.org/products/.."

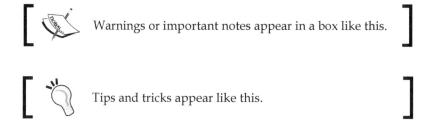

Warnings or important notes appear in a box like this.

Tips and tricks appear like this.

Reader feedback

Feedback from our readers is always welcome. Let us know what you think about this book—what you liked or disliked. Reader feedback is important for us as it helps us develop titles that you will really get the most out of.

To send us general feedback, simply e-mail feedback@packtpub.com, and mention the book's title in the subject of your message.

If there is a topic that you have expertise in and you are interested in either writing or contributing to a book, see our author guide at www.packtpub.com/authors.

Customer support

Now that you are the proud owner of a Packt book, we have a number of things to help you to get the most from your purchase.

Downloading the example code

You can download the example code files for this book from your account at
`http://www.packtpub.com`. If you purchased this book elsewhere, you can
visit `http://www.packtpub.com/support` and register to have the files e-mailed
directly to you.

You can download the code files by following these steps:

1. Log in or register to our website using your e-mail address and password.
2. Hover the mouse pointer on the **SUPPORT** tab at the top.
3. Click on **Code Downloads & Errata**.
4. Enter the name of the book in the **Search** box.
5. Select the book for which you're looking to download the code files.
6. Choose from the drop-down menu where you purchased this book from.
7. Click on **Code Download**.

You can also download the code files by clicking on the **Code Files** button on the
book's webpage at the Packt Publishing website. This page can be accessed by
entering the book's name in the **Search** box. Please note that you need to be
logged in to your Packt account.

Once the file is downloaded, please make sure that you unzip or extract the folder
using the latest version of:

- WinRAR / 7-Zip for Windows
- Zipeg / iZip / UnRarX for Mac
- 7-Zip / PeaZip for Linux

Downloading the color images of this book

We also provide you with a PDF file that has color images of the screenshots/diagrams
used in this book. The color images will help you better understand the changes in
the output. You can download this file from `https://www.packtpub.com/sites/`
`default/files/downloads/RaspberryPiByExample_ColorImages.pdf`.

Errata

Although we have taken every care to ensure the accuracy of our content, mistakes do happen. If you find a mistake in one of our books—maybe a mistake in the text or the code—we would be grateful if you could report this to us. By doing so, you can save other readers from frustration and help us improve subsequent versions of this book. If you find any errata, please report them by visiting http://www.packtpub.com/submit-errata, selecting your book, clicking on the **Errata Submission Form** link, and entering the details of your errata. Once your errata are verified, your submission will be accepted and the errata will be uploaded to our website or added to any list of existing errata under the Errata section of that title.

To view the previously submitted errata, go to https://www.packtpub.com/books/content/support and enter the name of the book in the search field. The required information will appear under the **Errata** section.

Piracy

Piracy of copyrighted material on the Internet is an ongoing problem across all media. At Packt, we take the protection of our copyright and licenses very seriously. If you come across any illegal copies of our works in any form on the Internet, please provide us with the location address or website name immediately so that we can pursue a remedy.

Please contact us at copyright@packtpub.com with a link to the suspected pirated material.

We appreciate your help in protecting our authors and our ability to bring you valuable content.

Questions

If you have a problem with any aspect of this book, you can contact us at questions@packtpub.com, and we will do our best to address the problem.

1

Introduction to Raspberry Pi and Python

One can learn about topics in computer science in an easy way with the Raspberry Pi and Python. The Raspberry Pi family of single-board computers uses Python as the preferred development language. Using Raspberry Pi and Python to learn programming and computer science-related concepts is one of the best ways to start your journey in this amazing world of computers that is full of creative possibilities. We will explore these possibilities in this book.

We will commence our journey in this chapter by getting ourselves familiar with the following topics:

- Single-board computers
- Raspberry Pi
- Raspbian
- Setting up Raspberry Pi
- Basics of Python
- Turtle programming with Python

Single-board computers

A single-board computer system is a complete computer on a single circuit board. The board includes a processor(s), RAM, input/output (I/O), and networking ports for interfacing devices. Unlike traditional computer systems, a single-board computer is not modular and its hardware cannot be upgraded as it is integrated on the board itself. Single-board computers are used as low-cost computers in academia, research, and embedded systems. The use of single-board computers in embedded systems is quite prevalent and many individuals and organizations have developed and released fully functional products based on single-board computers.

The Microcomputer Trainer MMD-1 designed by John Titus in 1976 is the first true single-board microcomputer that was based on the Intel C8080A. It was called **dyna -micro** in the prototyping phase, and the production units were called **MMD-1** (short for **Mini Micro Designer 1**).

Popular single-board computers available in the market include but are not limited to Raspberry Pi, Banana Pro, BeagleBone Black, and Cubieboard. The following images are of the front view of BeagleBone Black, Banana Pro, and Cubieboard 4, respectively:

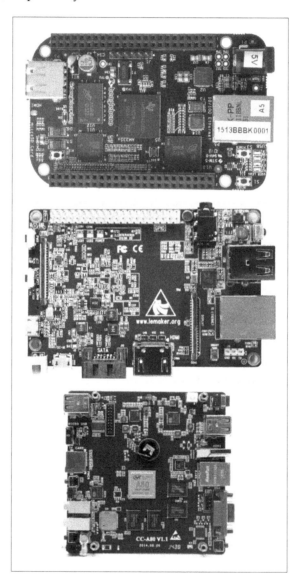

Raspberry Pi

The Raspberry Pi is a series of low-cost, palm-sized single-board computers developed by Raspberry Pi Foundation in the UK. The intention behind the creation of the Raspberry Pi is to promote the teaching of basic computer skills in schools, which it serves very well. Raspberry Pi has expanded its footprint well beyond its intended purpose by penetrating the embedded systems market and computer science research.

 This is the home page of Raspberry Pi Foundation: http://www.raspberrypi.org.

The Raspberry Pi is manufactured with licensed agreements with Newark element14, RS Components, Allied Electronics, and Egoman. These companies manufacture and sell the Raspberry Pi. The hardware is the same across all manufacturers.

The following table displays the URLs of the manufacturers' websites, where you can shop for Pi and related items online:

Manufacturer	Website
Newark element14	http://www.newark.com
RS Components	http://uk.rs-online.com
Egoman	http://www.egoman.com.cn
Allied Electronics	http://www.alliedelec.com

You can also shop for Pi and the other third-party add-ons at the following links:

* http://shop.pimoroni.com
* http://www.adafruit.com

Raspberry Pi models

The following are, at the time of writing this, the major models of Raspberry Pi:

* Model A (not in production; discontinued in favor of the production of later and upgraded models)
* Model A+ (currently in production and available for purchase)
* Model B (available for purchase but not in production)
* Model B+ (currently in production and available for purchase)
* Raspberry Pi 2 Model B (currently in production and available for purchase)

Check out the **Product** page of Raspberry Pi at
http://www.raspberrypi.org/products/.

Additionally, Raspberry Pi is also available in a more flexible form factor intended for industrial and embedded applications. It is known as **Compute Module**. A Compute Module prototyping kit is also made available by the foundation.

 Check out the following URLs for the Compute Module and Compute Module development kit, respectively:
http://www.raspberrypi.org/products/compute-module/
http://www.raspberrypi.org/products/compute-module-development-kit/

The following table compares the currently available models of Pi:

	Model A	Model B	Model B+	Pi 2 Model B
SOC (System on a chip)	Broadcom BCM2835(CPU, GPU, DSP, SDRAM, one USB port)			Broadcom.BCM2836 (CPU, GPU, DSP, SDRAM, one USB port)
CPU	700 MHz single-core ARM1176JZF-S			900 MHz quad-core ARM Cortex-A7
GPU	Broadcom videoCore IV @ 250 MHz			
Memory (shared with GPU)	256 MB SDRAM	516 MB SDRAM		1 GB SDRAM
USB 2.0 ports	1	2		4
On Board Storage	MicroSD slot	SD / MMC / SDIO card slot	MicroSD slot	
Networking	None	10/100.Mbit/s Ethernet, no Bluetooth or Wi-Fi		
Power Source	5V via Micro USB or GPIO Headers (Power supply through micro USB is recommended.)			
Power Ratings	200mA (1 W)	700mA (3.5 W)	600mA (3.5 W)	800mA (4 W)

The following image shows the top view of the Raspberry Pi Model B front:

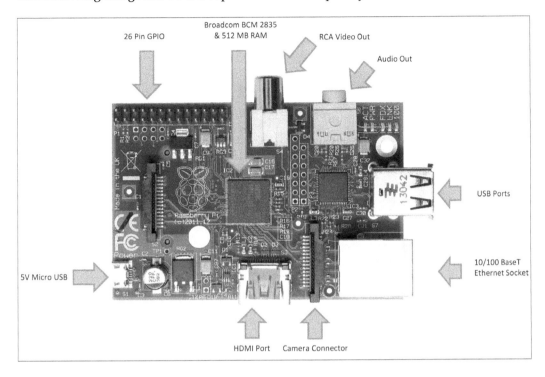

The following image shows the top view of the flip side of Raspberry Pi Model B:

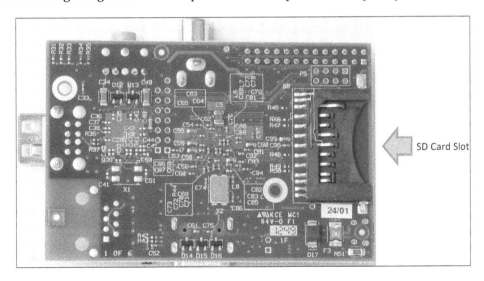

The following image shows the top view of the Raspberry Pi Model B+ front:

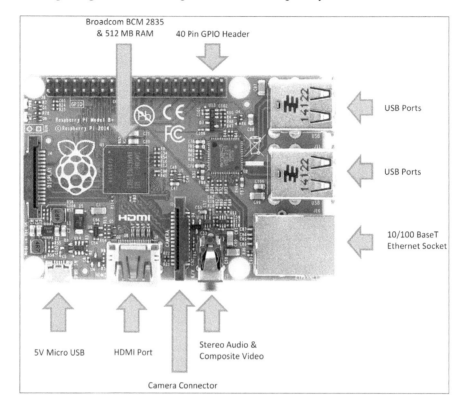

The following image shows the top view of the flip side of Raspberry Pi Model B+:

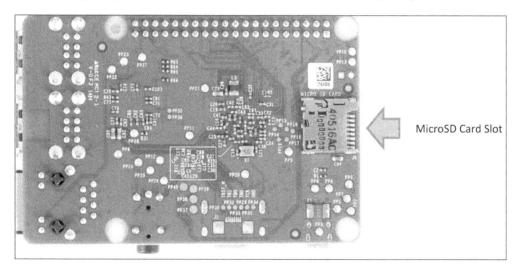

The following image shows the top view of the Raspberry Pi 2 Model B front. The location of the connectors and important ICs (integrated circuits) on the board is not different from Pi B+:

We will be using Raspberry Pi 2 Model B throughout this book. However, all the applications and programs in this book will work on all the models of Pi.

Operating systems

The Raspberry Pi primarily uses Unix-like Linux-kernel-based operating systems, such as variants of Debian and Fedora.

Raspberry Pi Models A, A+, B, and B+ are based on the ARM11 family chip, which runs on the ARMv6 instruction set. The ARMv6 instruction set does not support Ubuntu and Windows.

However, the recently launched Raspberry Pi 2 is based on ARM Cortex A7, which is capable of running Windows 10 and Ubuntu (Snappy Core). The following operating systems are officially supported by all the models of Raspberry Pi and are available for download at the download page:

- Raspbian: We will be using this with Raspberry Pi throughout the book
- OpenELEC
- Pidora (Fedora Remix)
- RASPBMC
- RISC OS

 Windows 10 and Ubuntu are only supported by the recently launched Pi 2.

Raspbian

Raspbian is an unofficial variant of Debian armhf (ARM Hard Float) compiled for *hard float* code that will run on Raspberry Pi computers. It is a free operating system based on Debian optimized for the Raspberry Pi hardware.

 To know more about Raspbian, visit http://www.raspbian.org/.

Setting up the Raspberry Pi

We need the following hardware to set up a Pi.

- Raspberry Pi 2 Model B (hereafter, this will be referred only as Pi).
- Power Supply: A micro USB power supply.

Considering that we are going for slightly power-intensive usage of our Pi (such as connecting Pi Camera, webcam, and third-party sensors for Pi), a 5V 2A power supply is recommended. The micro USB pin is shown in the following image:

 You can find a similar one online at http://www.adafruit.com/product/1995.

- A standard USB keyboard
- A MicroSD card and a MicroSD to SD card converter

  We need a minimum 4 GB Micro SD card.

- A USB mouse
- A monitor

  You can use either an HDMI monitor or a standard VGA monitor.

- A monitor connection cable and converter

  If you are using HDMI monitor, then an HDMI cable will be sufficient. If you are using a VGA monitor, then you need to use an HDMI to VGA converter with a VGA cable. Some special changes need to be made to the `/boot/config.txt` file if you're using a VGA monitor, which will be explained in the next section.

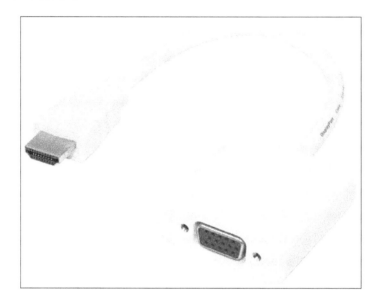

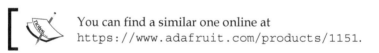

[You can find a similar one online at `https://www.adafruit.com/products/1151`.]

- A Windows, Linux, or Mac OS computer with a MicroSD card reader and an Internet connection

Preparing MicroSD card manually

This is the original way to install an OS into a MicroSD card, and many users, including me, still prefer it. It allows the SD card to be prepared manually before it is used and it allows easier access to configuration files such as `/boot/config.txt`, which we might have to modify in a few cases before booting up. The default Raspbian image consists of only two partitions, `BOOT` and `SYSTEM`, which will fit into a 2 GB card. However, I recommend that you use a minimum 4 GB card to be on safe side. Choosing an 8 GB card will be adequate for most of the applications we are going to develop in this book.

The following are the instructions for Windows users:

1. Download the Win32DiskImager installer, which is available at `http://sourceforge.net/projects/win32diskimager/files/latest/download` and then install it.

2. Download the installable version of WinZip, which is available at `http://www.winzip.com/prod_down.html`, and install it.

3. Go to `http://www.raspberrypi.org/downloads` and download the latest image of Raspbian. It will be a compressed file in the ZIP format and will need to be extracted.

4. Extract the ZIP file using WinZip. The extracted file will be in the `.img` format.

5. Insert the microSD card into the card reader and plug the card reader into the computer. Many computers nowadays have an inbuilt SD card reader. In this case, you will need to insert the microSD card into the microSD to SD card converter and insert it into the computer's inbuilt SD card reader. MicroSD to SD card converters usually come bundled with microSD cards in the same package. If that's not the case, then you will have to procure it separately.

6. Run `Win32DiskImager.exe` and write the image onto the SD card:

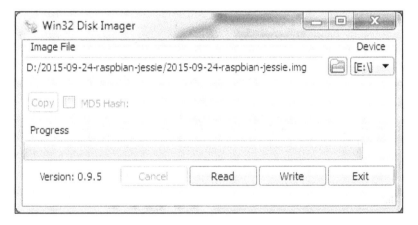

You might receive the following message if the card reader's write protection is on:

7. Toggle the write protection notch and try again. You will see the following message:

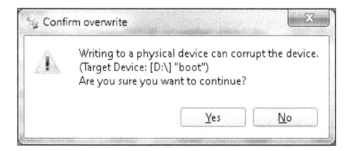

8. Click on **Yes** and it will start writing the image file to the microSD card:

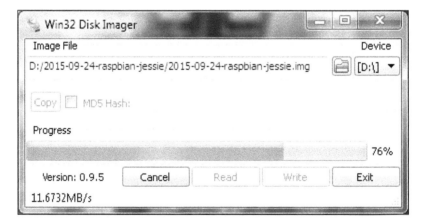

9. Once the image is successfully written, it will display the following message:

If you are using Linux, then you can find the instructions at
https://www.raspberrypi.org/documentation/
installation/installing-images/linux.md.

If you are using Mac OS, then you can find the instructions
at https://www.raspberrypi.org/documentation/
installation/installing-images/mac.md.

If you have an HDMI monitor, then skip this step. This additional step is required only if you are planning to use a VGA monitor in place of an HDMI monitor.

Browse the microSD card on the computer. Locate and open config.txt. We have to edit the file in order to enable proper display on the VGA monitor.

By default, the commented options (which have # at the beginning) are disabled. We are enabling this option by uncommenting this line, that is, by removing # from the beginning of the commented line. This is what you need to do:

1. Change #disable_overscan=1 to disable_overscan=1.
2. Change #hdmi_force_hotplug=1 to hdmi_force_hotplug=1.
3. Change #hdmi_group=1 to hdmi_group=2.
4. Change #hdmi_mode=1 to hdmi_mode=16.
5. Change #hdmi_drive=2 to hdmi_drive=2.
6. Change #config_hdmi_boost-4 to config_hdmi_boost=4.
7. Save the file.

Booting up our Pi for the first time

Let's boot up our Pi for the first time with the microSD card:

1. Insert the microSD card into the microSD card slot of the Pi.

2. Connect the Pi to the HDMI monitor. If you are connecting the VGA monitor, connect it using the HDMI to VGA converter.

3. Connect the USB mouse and the USB keyboard.

4. Connect the Pi to a power supply using the micro USB power cable. Make sure the power is switched off at this point.

5. Check all the connections once and then switch on the power supply of the Pi.

At this stage, our Pi will start booting up. You will see a green light on the Pi board blinking. This means that it's working! Now, there are few more things we need to do before we can really start using our Pi. Once it boots up, it will show the desktop as follows:

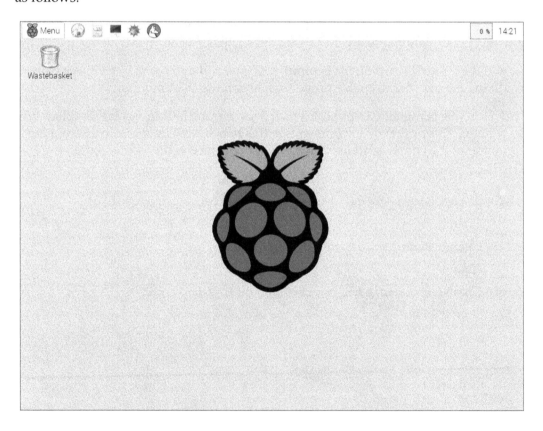

Once the desktop is visible, go to **Menu | Accessories | lxterminal**. Then, type `sudo raspi-config`. A text-based menu, such as the following, will appear:

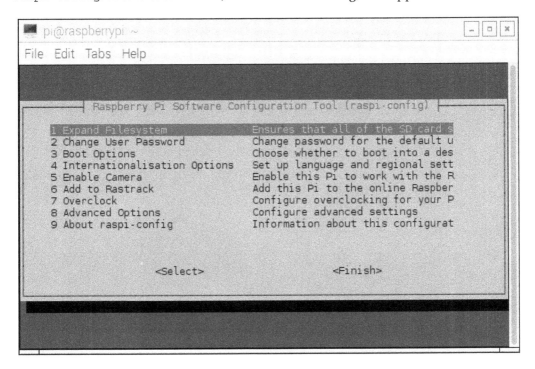

Perform the following steps. We need to use arrow keys and the *Enter* key to select options in the text-based menu. Press *Enter* to select a menu item. Also, we can use the *Tab* key to directly go to the **Select** and **Finish** buttons:

1. Select **Expand Filesystem**.

2. In **Boot Options**, select **B4 Desktop Autologin**, as shown in the following screenshot:

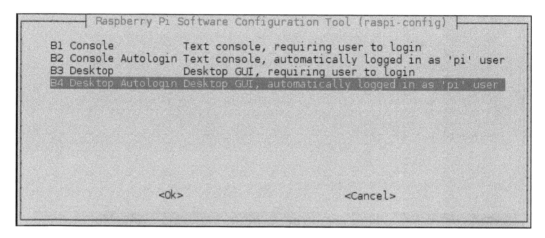

 The default username is `pi` and the password is `raspberry`. We need it when we don't choose any of the preceding autologin options. We can change this password from the second option in the `raspi-config` menu.

We can also choose to boot to the console by selecting any of the first two options in the preceding menu. The default shell of Raspbian is Bash. We can confirm it by typing the following command:

`echo $SHELL`

We can always go to the graphical desktop from the Command Prompt by typing the `startx` command in the console.

3. Go to **Internationalisation Options** | **Change Timezone**.

4. Go to **Internationalisation Options** | **Change Keyboard Layout** | **Change it to US** (the default is **UK**).

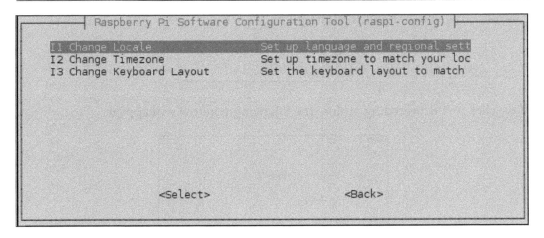

5. Select **Enable Camera**.

6. Select **Advanced Options**.

7. Under this option, select **Memory Split** and enter 64MB for GPU.

This option decides how much RAM is used by the **GPU** (**Graphics Processor Unit**). The more RAM is allocated to the GPU, the more intensive graphics processing can be done. 64 MB is a good value for most graphics purposes.

Once all these options are modified, select **Finish**. This will prompt for a reboot of the Pi. Choose **Yes** and let it reboot. Once rebooted, it will automatically take us to the Raspbian Desktop again.

You can always invoke the raspi-config tool from Command Prompt with the following command and change the settings:

```
sudo raspi-config
```

Shutting down and rebooting Pi safely

In the Raspbian menu, there are options to shut down and reboot the Pi.

If we click on the following **Menu** button on the desktop, it will display multiple options:

The following image shows the last option:

If we click on the preceding option, the following window will appear:

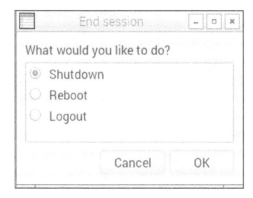

Also, from Command Prompt LXTerminal, we can shut down Pi safely by issuing the following command:

```
sudo shutdown -h now
```

An alternative command for this is as follows:

```
sudo halt
```

You can reboot Pi with the following command:

```
sudo reboot
```

Updating the Pi

Now we have a working Pi running on the Raspbian OS. Let's update our Pi. Make sure you have a working wired or wireless Internet connection with reasonable speed for this activity:

1. Connect your Pi to an Internet modem or router with an Ethernet cable or plug in the Wi-Fi dongle to one of the USB ports.

2. Run the following command to restart the networking service:

   ```
   sudo service networking restart
   ```

3. Make sure that your Raspberry Pi is connected to the Internet by typing the following command:

```
ping -c4 www.google.com
```

4. `apt` (Advanced Package Tool) is the utility used to install and remove software in Debian and its variants. We need to use it to update our Pi software.

5. Run the following commands in a sequence:

   ° `sudo apt-get update`: This command synchronizes the package list from the source. Indexes of all the packages are refreshed. This command must be issued before we issue the `upgrade` command.

   ° `sudo apt-get upgrade`: This command will install the newest versions of all the already installed software. Any obsolete packages/utilities are not removed automatically. If any software is in its newest version, then it's left as it is.

   ° `sudo rpi-update`: This command is used to upgrade the firmware. The kernel and firmware are installed as a Debian package, and so they will also get updates. These packages are updated infrequently after extensive testing.

   ° `sudo reboot`: This will reboot the computer.

Getting started with Python

Python is a high-level general-purpose programming language. It supports multiple programming paradigms, such as object-oriented programming, imperative programming, functional programming, procedural programming, aspect-oriented programming, and metaprogramming. It has a dynamic type system, automatic memory management, and a large standard library to carry out various tasks. It emphasizes code readability, and its syntax allows you to carry out tasks in fewer lines of code than other programming languages, such as C or C++.

Python was conceived and implemented by Guido van Rossum at CWI in the Netherlands as a successor to the ABC language, capable of exception handling and interfacing with the Amoeba operating system platform. Van Rossum is Python's principal author, and he continues to have the central role in deciding the direction of Python. He has been endowed with the title **benevolent dictator for life** (**BDFL**) by the worldwide Python community.

The core philosophy of the Python programming language is mentioned in this URL: `https://www.python.org/dev/peps/pep-0020/`; its first few lines are as follows:

"Beautiful is better than ugly.

Explicit is better than implicit.

Simple is better than complex.

Complex is better than complicated.

Flat is better than nested.

Sparse is better than dense.

Readability counts."

Python is the preferred programming language for the Raspberry Pi family of computers. Its interpreter comes preinstalled with Raspbian, and there is no need for any additional installation to get started with code. It is recommended that you have chapter wise directories for the code examples presented in this book, as shown in the following diagram:

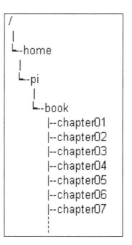

Let's get started with Python. Open Raspbian's Command Prompt LXTerminal. It is located as a shortcut on the taskbar. Alternately, we can find it by navigating to **Menu | Accessories | Terminal**. We can start Python in interactive mode by typing `python` in the prompt and then pressing the *Enter* key. It will take us to the Python interactive shell, as follows:

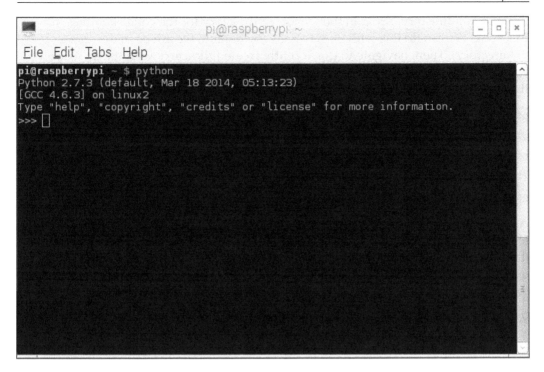

Now type the following lines and press *Enter*:

```
print "Hello World!"
```

The output will be as follows:

```
Python 2.7.3 (default, Mar 18 2014, 05:13:23)
[GCC 4.6.3] on linux2
Type "help", "copyright", "credits" or "license" for more information.
>>> print "Hello World!"
Hello World!
```

Congrats! We have started with Python programming. The interactive mode of Python is suitable for small programs. Press *Ctrl + D* to exit the interactive shell. For large and code-intensive projects, it's recommended that you use Python in script mode. In this book, we will be using Python in script mode unless specified explicitly. Let's look at how to use Python in script mode.

Create a subdirectory, book, in the /home/pi directory for the code examples in this book. We can do this with mkdir book (by default, we are be in the /home/pi directory). Then, navigate to this recently created directory with the cd book command. We can verify our current directory with the pwd command. It returns the current directory as follows:

```
pi@raspberrypi ~ $ mkdir book
pi@raspberrypi ~ $ cd book
pi@raspberrypi ~/book $ pwd
/home/pi/book
pi@raspberrypi ~/book $
```

As discussed earlier, we need to keep the code of each chapter in separate directories for better organization. Now, create the chapter01 directory for this chapter in the current book directory using mkdir chapter01. Navigate to this with cd chapter01. At the beginning of each chapter, we are required to create a directory for the chapter under /home/pi/book for the code examples of that chapter.

We will now create a script file for our code and run it.

Use the Nano text editor to create and edit script files. If we type nano prog1.py, then Nano will open prog1.py for editing if it already exists in the current directory; otherwise, it will create a new file with the name prog1.py. You can exit the Nano editor by pressing *Ctrl + X*.

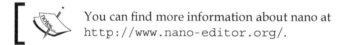

You can find more information about nano at http://www.nano-editor.org/.

Alternatively, you can use the Leafpad text editor. We can find it by navigating to **Menu | Accessories**. Or, we can invoke it from Command Prompt with the leafpad prog1.py command.

Finally, you can also use vim, but you will need to install it by running the following command:

```
sudo apt-get install vim
```

This is the link for an interactive tutorial on vim: http://www.openvim.com/.

```
print "Hello World!"
```

To run the preceding program, use the `python prog1.py` command, and the output will be as follows.

We will run all the other Python programs in this book in the same way.

Let's try some more examples to have more hands-on Python.

The following is the iterative program to calculate the factorial of a given positive integer:

```
def fact(n):
    num = 1
    while n >= 1:
        num = num * n
        n = n - 1
    return num


print (fact(10))
```

In the preceding program, `def fact(n)` is a user-defined function that accepts an argument. The logic used to calculate the factorial of a positive integer follows the definition and the function returns a calculated factorial. The last line of the program calls the factorial function and prints the returned output as follows:

```
pi@raspberrypi ~/book/chapter01 $ python prog2.py
3628800
```

The following is an iterative program for the Fibonacci series:

```
def fib(n):
    a=0
    b=1
    for i in range(n):
        temp=a
        a=b
        b=temp+b
    return a

for i in range (0,10):
    print (fib(i))
```

The preceding program prints the first 10 numbers in the Fibonacci series. A more "Pythonic" way of writing the same program, which eliminates the use of a temporary variable, is as follows:

```
def fib(n):
    a,b = 0,1
    for i in range(n):
        a,b = b,a+b
    return a

for i in range(0,10):
    print (fib(i))
```

The output of both of the preceding programs is the same and is as follows:

```
pi@raspberrypi ~/book/chapter01 $ python prog4.py
0
1
1
2
3
5
8
13
21
34
```

Turtle programming with Python

Turtle graphics is one of the best ways to learn programming for beginners. Originally, it was part of the Logo programming language, which was primarily used to introduce programming in schools. Python has the `turtle` module, which is an implementation of the same functionality provided by the original turtle. We can write programs with this module in a procedural as well as object-oriented way.

In Python, when we need to access a module that is not part of the current code, we need to import it. Over the course of the book, we will be importing various modules as and when needed, which will provide us with specific functionalities.

Let's get started with importing the `turtle` module, as shown here:

```
import turtle
```

The following code creates objects for turtle and the screen classes, respectively:

```
t=turtle.Turtle()
disp=turtle.Screen()
```

We will use the t.color() function with which we can set the pen and fill color, as follows:

```
t.color("black","yellow")
```

We will call the t.begin_fill() and t.end_fill() functions to have our shape filled with a fill color:

```
t.begin_fill()
t.end_fill()
```

The code to draw an actual shape we need will be in between these two function calls, as follows:

```
t.begin_fill()
while 1:
    t.forward(100)
    t.left(190)
    if abs(t.pos())<1:
        break
t.end_fill()
disp.exitonclick()
```

In the preceding code, t.forward() is used to move the turtle forward a specified distance, and t.left() is used to rotate the turtle left by 190 degrees. t.pos() returns the current coordinates of the turtle.

Finally, we use disp.exitonclick() to close the current output window when we click on the exit button.

 At the start, the turtle cursor is at (0,0) and is pointed toward the positive direction of the *x* axis (facing right).

The output of the program will be a cursor drawing the desired shape progressively, and it helps the programmer understand how the program is actually working. The final output of the preceding program is as follows:

 Detailed documentation for the turtle API can be found at https://docs.python.org/2/library/turtle.html.

Next, we will learn the concept of recursion. In terms of programming, recursion means calling the same block of code within itself. For a procedural and modular style of programming, this stands for calling a function or method within itself. Usually, this is done to break a big problem into similar problems with smaller input sizes and then collect the output of all these smaller problems to derive the output of the big problem. One of the best ways to see recursion at work is to visualize it using a turtle. We will now write a program to draw a fractal tree using recursion.

First, we start by importing the required libraries, as follows:

```
import turtle
import random
```

We need the `random` library for the `randint()` function, which returns a random integer in the provided range. This is needed to make our generated tree seem different every time. Then, we will define a function to draw a part of the tree recursively:

```
def fractal_tree(b_len,t):
    if b_len > 5:
        temp=random.randint(1, b_len)
        temp_angle = random.randint(1, 25)
        t.forward(temp)
        t.right(temp_angle)
        fractal_tree(b_len-10,t)
        t.left(2 * temp_angle)
        fractal_tree(b_len-10,t)
        t.right(temp_angle)
        t.backward(temp)
```

In the preceding program, we are calling the same function twice in order to draw the further branches of the tree. If the `b_len` parameter is less than or equal to 5, then it will be a leaf (which means that the function will not be called again); else, the recursion will continue. We are randomizing the angle and length of the movement of the turtle while drawing the branches here; otherwise, the tree will be symmetrical, which is very unlikely in real life. The combination of `t.forward()`, `t.backward()`, `t.left()`, and `t.right()` ensures that at the end of each function call, the turtle cursor is at the same position as where it started.

Finally, we write the routine to call this recursive function:

```
t=turtle.Turtle()
disp=turtle.Screen()
t.left(90)
t.up()
t.backward(100)
t.down()
t.color("green")
fractal_tree(120,t)
disp.exitonclick()
```

The cursor does not draw the movements between the t.up() and t.down() function calls. In the preceding code, we are moving the cursor downward by 100 positions so that the tree should fit in the turtle graphics window. When we call fractal_tree() with 120 as the argument, it takes more than 30 minutes due to the high degree of recursion. The output of the preceding program is as follows:

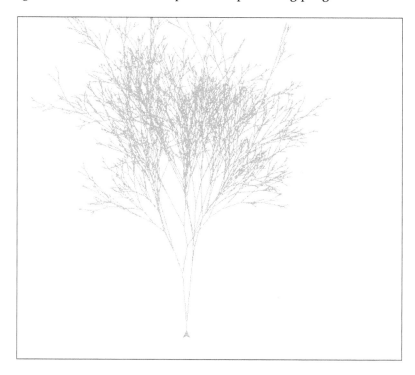

Summary

In this chapter, we learned about the background of Raspberry Pi and Python. We understood the details of the different models of Pi. We learned how to set up the Raspberry Pi for programming. We also performed some hands-on Python programs. Then, we learned some graphics programming with the turtle library. This got us started with the Pi and the Python programming language, which we will be using throughout the rest of the book.

In the next chapter, we will learn how to play and program minecraft-pi.

2
Minecraft Pi

In the previous chapter, we learned how to set up the Pi and looked at Python and turtle modules briefly. In this chapter, we are going to explore the Pi version of a popular computer game, *Minecraft*. We will also learn how to program Minecraft with Python as the programming interface and use it to script user actions and build wonderful things.

We will cover the following topics in this chapter:

- Introducing Minecraft Pi
- Playing Minecraft Pi
- Programming Minecraft Pi with Python

Introduction to Minecraft Pi

Minecraft is a very popular open world game. Like all other open world games, the player can freely explore the virtual world in a Minecraft Pi game. Minecraft was created by Markus Persson, and the game was later developed and published by the company Mojang, which is a Microsoft Game Studios subsidiary now. Jens Bergensten is the current lead designer and lead developer for the game. The alpha version of the game was released for PCs in 2009, and the complete version was released in 2011. The game is available for various platforms, which include PCs, Linux, Mac OS, iOS, Android, PlayStation, Xbox, and Raspberry Pi.

[You can get more information on Minecraft at
https://minecraft.net/.]

The version of this game for the Raspberry Pi is known as Minecraft Pi, and it was released in 2013. It was developed by Aron Nieminen and Daniel Frisk. Minecraft Pi focuses on the creative and building aspect of the game and does not include gathering resources and combat.

Playing Minecraft Pi

Minecraft Pi comes preinstalled in the latest version of Raspbian. So, there is no need for an additional installation. Minecraft Pi can be found by navigating to **Menu | Games**. Alternatively, we can start it by typing `minecraft-pi` in `lxterminal`. The following screen will appear once we start the game:

Click on the **Start Game** button. Then, the following window will appear:

Click on **Create New** and it will start generating a new world for the gameplay:

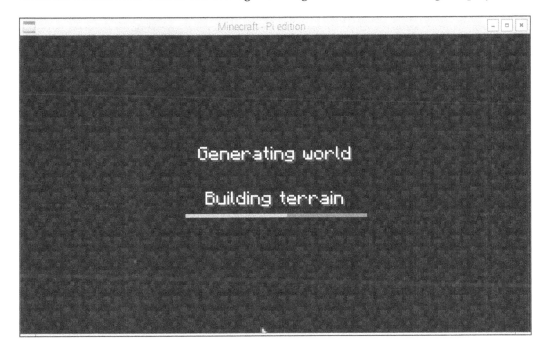

Once the new world for the gameplay is generated, the player character is placed in the virtual world. The default view in the game is the first-person view. It will look as follows:

 In Minecraft Pi, a new world is randomly generated in a procedural manner. This means that the world is randomly created with the algorithm rather than using predetermined components. So, no two worlds in Minecraft Pi will be the same. You can learn more about procedural generation from https://en.wikipedia.org/wiki/Procedural_generation.

We can switch from the first-person view to the third-person view by pressing the *Esc* key or by clicking on the following button for a view change:

Once this button is clicked on, it will change to the following button:

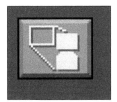

At this point, once we return to the game by pressing the *Esc* key or clicking on the **Back to game** button, we will see our Minecraft Pi character in the third person, as follows:

We can change this view to the first person view again by following the preceding steps.

Movement control in Minecraft Pi

We can use a mouse to look around and also make use of the following keys for the movement:

Key	Action
W	Forward
S	Backward
A	Left
D	Right
Spacebar	Jump
Double spacebar	Fly or fall

Like most first/third-person games, movement is controlled by *WSAD* keys on the keyboard. The character jumps if spacebar is pressed once. If we hit spacebar twice, the character is lifted in the air, as shown in the following screenshot:

At this point, *WSAD* keys can be used to fly in the air. We can increase the altitude by pressing spacebar while flying. The following screenshot shows the game world view from a higher altitude:

If spacebar is pressed twice while flying, then the character will fall on the ground. While the character is falling, if we press spacebar twice, it will stop falling.

Action control in Minecraft Pi

By default, the player character starts with a sword in hand. If we right-click with the sword in hand, it will remove the block in front of the character.

There is a quick draw panel at the bottom of the screen, as follows:

Any item can be selected by scrolling the mouse wheel or using the numbers on the keyboard. The quick draw panel always hold eight items, and the current item in the hand is highlighted as follows:

More items can be accessed by pressing the *E* key. This will open the inventory, as follows:

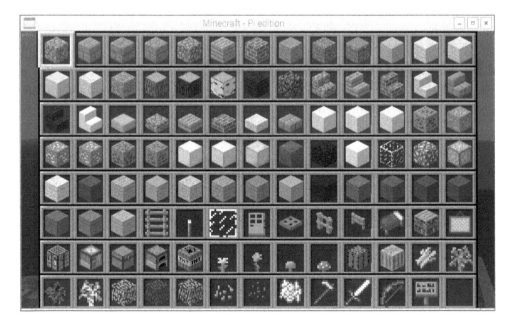

Items in the inventory can be navigated by *WSAD* keys. While the inventory is open, if the *Esc* key is pressed, it will cancel the inventory without choosing an item. Items in the inventory can be chosen by clicking on the item, and the item will be added to the quick draw panel as well as the character's hand, as follows:

With a block in the character's hand, right-clicking will place the block in front of the character and left-clicking will remove it. The number of blocks available to the player character is infinite.

Minecraft Pi features a creative mode, so the character does not take environmental damage (for example, when the character falls, it does not die) and is not affected by hunger. This game mode helps players focus on building and creating large projects.

Unlike other editions of Minecraft, Minecraft Pi does not feature any other gameplay modes.

Other controls in Minecraft Pi

When a game is running, pressing the *Tab* key will take the focus away from the game, and the mouse cursor will be freed to enable interaction with other windows on the desktop. Pressing *Esc* will pause the game and will take us to the game menu, where we can toggle views (as seen earlier), enable/disable sound, and quit the main window.

> Now, with all this information on the movements and the actions in the Minecraft Pi virtual game world, try to create a few things before continuing with the remainder of this chapter.

Python programming for Minecraft Pi

Minecraft Pi comes with the Python programming interface. This means that it's possible to script the action of a character in the game using Python. In this section, we will learn how to use Python programming to script the character actions as well as create amazing effects in the Minecraft world.

Start Minecraft Pi and create the world. Once it's done, while the game is running, free the mouse by pressing the *Tab* key and opening lxterminal. Create the /home/pi/book/chapter02 directory. Navigate to the directory and write the following code in the prog1.py file:

```
import mcpi.minecraft as minecraft

mc = minecraft.Minecraft.create()

mc.postToChat("Hello Minecraft World!")
```

The preceding program first imports the Minecraft Pi Python API. The second statement creates the connection to Minecraft, and the third statement posts the message to the game chat.

Run the preceding code; the following is its output:

Let's take a look at some of the most important functions of the Minecraft Pi Python API.

We can see the player's current coordinates in the game window in the top-left corner of the window. We can retrieve these coordinates with getPos(). The following is the code to retrieve the player character's current coordinates and print them:

```
import mcpi.minecraft as minecraft
mc = minecraft.Minecraft.create()
cur_pos = mc.player.getPos()
print cur_pos.x ; print cur_pos.y ; print cur_pos.z
```

This will print the current coordinates to the screen. Alternatively, the following syntax can be used to achieve this:

```
import mcpi.minecraft as minecraft
mc = minecraft.Minecraft.create()
cur_x , cur_y , cur_z = mc.player.getPos()
print cur_x ; print cur_y ; print cur_z
```

The setPos() function can be used to set the character's position. We need to pass the desired coordinates of the character to this function, as follows:

```
import mcpi.minecraft as minecraft
mc = minecraft.Minecraft.create()
cur_x , cur_y , cur_z = mc.player.getPos()
mc.player.setPos(cur_x+10, cur_y, cur_z)
```

The preceding code will displace the character by 10 blocks in the *x* axis.

The following code will set the character position 100 blocks higher than the current position, and as a result, the character will start falling:

```
mc.player.setPos(cur_x, cur_y + 100 , cur_z)
```

We can place the blocks of our choice with the setBlock() function. We need to pass the coordinates of the block (the first three arguments) and the type of the block (the fourth argument) we need to set to this function as follows:

```
import mcpi.minecraft as minecraft
import mcpi.block as block
mc = minecraft.Minecraft.create()
cur_x , cur_y , cur_z = mc.player.getPos()
mc.setBlock(cur_x + 1 , cur_y , cur_z , block.ICE.id )
```

You will find an ice block placed in front of you. If you do not find the block, then try to look around; it will be just beside or behind you.

Some blocks (such as wool and wood) have additional properties. We can pass this additional property as the fifth argument to the function for the wool and wood block types. The following code creates a column of a wool block with all the possible colors:

```
import mcpi.minecraft as minecraft
import mcpi.block as block
mc = minecraft.Minecraft.create()
cur_x , cur_y , cur_z = mc.player.getPos()

for i in range (0 , 15):
    mc.setBlock(cur_x + 1 , cur_y + i , cur_z , block.WOOL.id, i )
```

Run the preceding code and check the output for yourself.

We can use `setBlocks()` to place multiple blocks for a given volume. The following example places multiple gold blocks:

```
import mcpi.minecraft as minecraft
import mcpi.block as block
mc = minecraft.Minecraft.create()
cur_x , cur_y , cur_z = mc.player.getPos()

mc.setBlocks(cur_x + 1 , cur_y + 1 , cur_z + 1 , cur_x + 6 ,
cur_y + 6 , cur_z  + 6 , block.GOLD_BLOCK.id )
```

We can also use mathematical equations to draw geometric shapes in the game world. Now we know that `setBlock()` is used to place a single block. We can use this function in a single `for` loop to create a line of blocks. Calling this function in a double `for` loop will set a two-dimensional geometric shape. We can further extend this by introducing one more `for` loop. This will create a three-dimensional shape. The following code places a golden sphere near the player's position. We will place the gold block in the positions where the coordinates satisfy the equation of the sphere with a radius of 10 blocks:

```
import mcpi.minecraft as minecraft
import mcpi.block as block

mc = minecraft.Minecraft.create()

r = 10

cur_x , cur_y , cur_z = mc.player.getPos()

for x in range(r*-1,r):
  for y in range(r*-1, r):
    for z in range(r*-1,r):
      if x**2 + y**2 + z**2 < r**2:
        mc.setBlock(cur_x + x, cur_y + ( y + 20 ) , cur_z - (
        z + 20 ) , block.GOLD_BLOCK)
```

The following is the output of the preceding program:

The following code places a gold block below the player's current position until the execution of the code is terminated by pressing *Ctrl + C*:

```
import mcpi.minecraft as minecraft
import mcpi.block as block
import time

mc = minecraft.Minecraft.create()

while 1:
    cur_x, cur_y , cur_z = mc.player.getPos()
    mc.setBlock(cur_x,cur_y-1,cur_z,block.GOLD_BLOCK.id)
    time.sleep(0.1)
```

The following is the output of the preceding code:

Now, we will conclude the chapter with some explosions. We can place a TNT block near us. It can be activated by left-clicking while holding the sword in hand. It will explode in a few seconds. The explosion will destroy some blocks in the blast radius:

```
cur_x, cur_y , cur_z = mc.player.getPos()
mc.setBlocks(cur_x+1,cur_y,cur_z, block.TNT.id,1)
This can be made more spectacular by placing multiple TNT blocks,
as follows:
import mcpi.minecraft as minecraft
import mcpi.block as block

mc = minecraft.Minecraft.create()

cur_x, cur_y , cur_z = mc.player.getPos()
mc.setBlocks(cur_x+1,cur_y,cur_z,cur_x+4,cur_y+3,
cur_z+3,block.TNT.id,1)
```

Once blocks are placed, activate the TNT block by the sword. The following is the screenshot of an explosion after activating the TNT blocks placed by the preceding code:

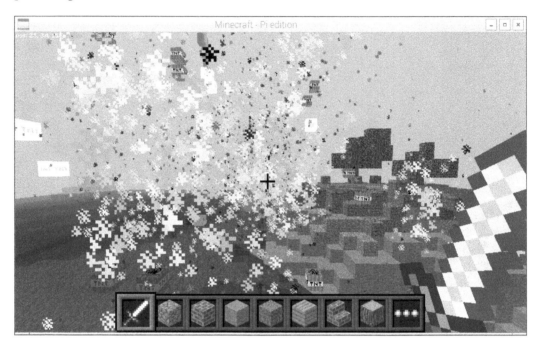

 The detailed Minecraft Pi Python API can be found at `http://www.stuffaboutcode.com/p/minecraft-api-reference.html`.

Summary

In this chapter, we got ourselves familiarized with the Minecraft Pi gameplay and learned how to program it using the Python API. We learned how to place and remove a block. Also, we implemented the code required to create some wonderful geometric shapes. In the end, we learned how to activate and explode TNT blocks to blow the large areas in the in-game world.

In the next chapter, we will learn how to use the Pygame library in order to create a game for the Pi.

3
Building Games with PyGame

In the previous chapter, we learned how to get started with Minecraft on Raspberry Pi and how to play it and use Python to manipulate things. Continuing with the same theme, we will now take a look at a gaming library in Python called PyGame and also learn how to create simple games with it. In this chapter, we will go through the following topics:

- Introducing PyGame
- Drawing a fractal tree
- Building a simple snake game

Introducing PyGame

PyGame is a set of Python modules designed for the writing of video games. It is built on top of the existing **Simple DirectMedia (SDL)** library, and it works with multiple backends, such as OpenGL, DirectX, X11, and so on. It was built with the intention of making game programming easier and faster without getting into the low-level C code that was traditionally used to achieve good real-time performance. It is also very flexible and comes with many operating systems. It is very fast as it can use multiple core CPUs very easily and also use optimized C and assembly code for core functions.

PyGame was built to replace PySDL after its development was discontinued. Originally written by Pete Shinners, it is a community project from 2004 and is released under the open source free software GNU's lesser general public license. Since it is very simple to use and is open source, it has a lot of members in the international community and so it enjoys access to a lot of resources that other libraries may lack. There are many tutorials that can build different games with PyGame. It contains the following modules

Module	The description
cdrom	Manages CD-ROM devices and audio playback
cursors	Loads cursor images and includes standard cursors
display	Controls the display window or screen
draw	Draws simple shapes onto a surface
event	Manages events and the event queue
font	Creates and renders Truetype fonts
image	Saves and loads images
joystick	Manages joystick devices
key	Manages the keyboard
mouse	Manages the mouse
movie	Used for the playback of MPEG movies
sndarray	Manipulates sounds with Numeric
surfarray	Manipulates images with Numeric
time	Controls timing
transform	Scales, rotates, and flips images

 For more information on the PyGame library, you can visit www.pygame.org.

Installing PyGame

PyGame usually comes installed with the latest Raspbian distribution, but if it isn't you can use the following command to install it:

```
sudo apt-get install python-pygame
```

Test your installation by opening a Python terminal by entering `python` in a regular terminal and pressing *Enter*. Now, execute the following command:

```
import pygame
```

Now that you have your system set up and you have hopefully checked out the PyGame website to explore its complete functionalities, we will move on to build the binary fractal tree to introduce you to the workings of PyGame. Let's begin!

Drawing a binary fractal tree

A binary fractal tree is defined recursively by binary branching. Typically, it consists of a trunk of length 1, which splits into two branches of decreasing or equal length, each of which makes an angle Q with the direction of the trunk. Furthermore, both of these branches are divided into two branches, each making an angle Q with the direction of its parent branch, and so on. Continuing in this way, we can infinitely make branches, and the collective diagram is called a **fractal tree**. The following diagram visually shows what such a fractal tree might look like:

Now, let's move on to the code and take a look at how such a fractal tree can be constructed with PyGame. Following this paragraph is the complete code, and we will go through it statement by statement in further paragraphs:

```python
import pygame
import math
import random
import time

width = 800
height = 600

pygame.init()
window = pygame.display.set_mode((width, height))
pygame.display.set_caption("Fractal Tree")
screen = pygame.display.get_surface()

def Fractal_Tree(x1, y1, theta, depth):
    if depth:
        rand_length=random.randint(1,10)
        rand_angle=random.randint(10,20)
        x2 = x1 + int(math.cos(math.radians(theta)) * depth * rand_
length)
    y2 = y1 + int(math.sin(math.radians(theta)) * depth * rand_length)
        if ( depth < 5 ):
            clr = ( 0 , 255 , 0 )
        else:
            clr = ( 255, 255 , 255 )
    pygame.draw.line(screen, clr , (x1, y1), (x2, y2), 2)
    Fractal_Tree(x2, y2, theta - rand_angle, depth - 1)
    Fractal_Tree(x2, y2, theta + rand_angle, depth - 1)

Fractal_Tree( (width/2), (height-10) , -90, 12)
pygame.display.flip()

while True:
    for event in pygame.event.get():
        if event.type == pygame.QUIT or event.type ==
        pygame.KEYDOWN:
            pygame.quit()
            exit(0)
```

Save the preceding code as `prog1.py` and then run the following:

```
python prog1.py
```

You will now get the following output:

If you increase the depth by 2 with a slight increase in the canvas area, the fractal tree now looks like this:

The new tree looks considerably denser and more branched out than the original tree.

Now, since you know what the output looks like, let's grab our magnifying glasses and sift through the program to understand how it works!

The first four lines are there to satisfy the dependencies required to build the program. These are PyGame, a math library, a library to generate random numbers, and a library to keep track of time for delay functions. Next, we specify the dimensions for the screen space required for our program.

The `pygame.init()` method initializes all the modules that were loaded as part of importing pygame in the first statement. It is required to be executed if you want to be able use any functionality of PyGame. The `display.set_mode()` method creates a new `Surface` object, which represents the area on the screen that is visible to the user. It takes a tuple consisting of the dimensions of the window as the argument: the `width` and `height` variables in this case. It is literally the canvas on which you can draw. Anything you do to this object will be shown to the user. Images and other objects are represented as PyGame objects, and you can overlay them on the the main surface. Then, we set the title of the window using the `caption()` method, and finally, the `screen` variable actually gets the object that the display is stored in. So now, our canvas is stored in the `screen` variable, and we will use it to make any changes to the canvas.

The `Fractal_Tree` function should be fairly easy to understand. It takes four arguments: the starting point of the branch (`X1`, `Y1`), the angle of the branch with respect to the positive *x* axis—which is a horizontal line going to your right when you look at the computer screen, and the depth of the fractal tree (which indicates the levels in the tree). It is called for the first time in the 28th line with appropriate arguments. You might notice that towards the end of the function, it calls itself using different arguments. These kinds of function are called recursive functions and are very useful in tasks where there is repetition and where the same task needs to be performed with minor differences.

If the depth is positive, it selects a random length and angle for the next branch by selecting a random integer from the `randint()` method of the random package. It then specifies the coordinates of the end of that branch, which are labeled `X2` and `Y2`. If the depth is less that 5, it selects the color of the line as green; otherwise, it is white. Here, it is important to understand that the color is represented in the RGB format. Hence, (`0`, `255`, `0`) means green. Similarly, (`255`, `0`, `0`) will be red. The three numbers in the tuple represent the intensity of RGB colors; hence, we can select any color using a mixture of these three intensities.

Finally, there is a recursive call to itself (`Fractal_tree`), and the program then draws the second level of the fractal tree and so on until the depth becomes zero. There are two recursive calls: one to draw the left branch and the other to draw the right branch. If you've noticed, the function isn't actually executed until the 28th line. And once it is executed, the complete pattern is drawn at once due to the recursiveness of the function, but it still isn't displayed. The next line, `pygame.display.flip()`, is responsible for displaying the drawn shapes on screen:

```
while True:
    for event in pygame.event.get():
If event.type == pygame.QUIT or event.type == pygame.KEYDOWN:
            pygame.quit()
            exit(0)
```

This block of code is there to ensure that PyGame quits properly and specifies how to shut down the program. The `event.get()` method clears the event queue so that you always get the last event that occurred. An event queue consists of all the key presses and mouse clicks that happen, and they are stored in a **Last In First Out (LIFO)** fashion. You will see this `while` loop in almost every PyGame program as it handles the exit of the program properly. If you are using IDLE, then not shutting down PyGame properly can cause it to hang. In this case, PyGame quits when `pygame.quit()` is executed. Finally, with `exit(0)`, Python also quits and closes the application.

As we are randomizing the length and the angle every time the function calls itself, no two branches will be exactly the same, giving it the appearance of the irregularity of real-life trees. By induction, no two trees will be same.

You can modify parts of this code to see for yourself how the tree behavior changes on changing a few variables, such as `theta` and `depth`. Now that we have completed all the basics of PyGame and can implement fairly complex problems, we are now ready to move on to a real challenge: making an actual game.

Building a snake game

Who doesn't remember the classic game called Snake, which involves a snake chasing a morsel of food? It is probably the very first game that you played as a child. The basic premise of the game is that you control a snake and lead it to a morsel of food. Every time the snake consumes that food, it grows by one unit length, and if the snake hits a boundary wall or itself, it dies. Now as you can imagine, the more you play the game, the longer the snake grows, which, consequently, makes it more difficult to control the snake. In some versions of the game, the speed of the snake also increases, making it even more difficult to control. There comes a point where you simply run out of screen space and the snake inevitably hits a wall or itself, and the game is over.

Here, we will learn how to build such a game. The basic logic of playing the game will be to have a moving rectangle, of which we know the leading point coordinates. This will be our snake. It will be controlled by the four arrow keys. The piece of food is initialized randomly on the screen. At each point of time, we will check whether the rectangle has hit the boundary wall or itself since we know the position of the snake at every point of time. If it has, then the program will exit. Let's now look at the code sectionwise; the code will be explained after each section:

```
from pygame.locals import *
import pygame
import random
import sys
import time

pygame.init()

fpsClock = pygame.time.Clock()

gameSurface = pygame.display.set_mode((800, 600))
pygame.display.set_caption('Pi Snake')

foodcolor = pygame.Color(0, 255, 0)
backgroundcolor = pygame.Color(255, 255, 255)
snakecolor = pygame.Color(0, 0, 0)
textcolor = pygame.Color(255, 0, 0)

snakePos = [120,240]
snakeSeg = [[120,240],[120,220]]
foodPosition = [400,300]
foodSpawned = 1
Dir = 'D'
changeDir = Dir
Score = 0
Speed = 5
SpeedCount = 0
```

Now, we will learn what each block of code does, but for brevity the very basics are skipped as we have already learned about them in the previous sections.

The first few lines before the `finish()` function initialize PyGame and set the game parameters. The `pygame.time.Clock()` function is used to track time within the game, and this is mostly used for frames per second, or FPS. While it seems somewhat trivial, FPS is very important and can be tweaked. We can increase or decrease the FPS to control the speed of the game. Going further into the code, we can choose options such as the screen size, the color of the snake, the starting position, the starting speed, and so on. The `snakePos` list variable has the head of the snake, and `snakeSeg` will contain the initial coordinates of the segment of the snake in a nested list. The first element contains the coordinates of the head, and the second element contains the coordinates of the tail. This block of code also defines the initial food position, the state of the food, the initial direction, the initial speed, and the initial player score:

```
def finish():
    finishFont = pygame.font.Font(None, 56)
    msg = "Game Over! Score = " + str(Score)
    finishSurf = finishFont.render(msg, True, textcolor)
    finishRect = finishSurf.get_rect()
    finishRect.midtop = (400, 10)
    gameSurface.blit(finishSurf, finishRect)
    pygame.display.flip()
    time.sleep(5)
    pygame.quit()
    exit(0)
```

The preceding block of code defines the finishing procedure for the game. As we will see in the following code, `finish()` is called when the snake either hits the walls or itself. In this, we first specify the message that we want to display and its properties, such as the font, and then we add the final score to it. Then, we render the message via the `render()` function, which operates on the `finishFont` variable. Then, we get a rectangle via `get_rect()`, and finally we draw those via the `blit()` function. When using PyGame, `blit()` is a very important function that allows us to draw one image on top of the other. In our case, this is very useful because it allows us to draw a bounding rectangle over the message that we show as a part of the ending of the game. Finally, we render our message on screen via the `display.flip()` function and after a delay of 5 seconds, we quit the game:

```
while 1:
    for event in pygame.event.get():
if event.type == QUIT:
pygame.quit()
            exit(0)
elif event.type == KEYDOWN:
if event.key == ord('d') or event.key == K_RIGHT:
```

```
changeDir = 'R'
if event.key == ord('a') or event.key == K_LEFT:
changeDir = 'L'
if event.key == ord('w') or event.key == K_UP:
changeDir = 'U'
if event.key == ord('s') or event.key == K_DOWN:
changeDir = 'D'
if event.key == K_ESCAPE:
pygame.event.post(pygame.event.Event(QUIT))
        pygame.quit()
        exit(0)

if changeDir == 'R' and not Dir == 'L':
Dir = changeDir
if changeDir == 'L' and not Dir == 'R':
Dir = changeDir
if changeDir == 'U' and not Dir == 'D':
Dir = changeDir
if changeDir == 'D' and not Dir == 'U':
Dir = changeDir

if Dir == 'R':
snakePos[0] += 20
if Dir == 'L':
snakePos[0] -= 20
if Dir == 'U':
snakePos[1] -= 20
if Dir == 'D':
snakePos[1] += 20
```

Then, we move on to the infinite `while` loop, which contains the bulk of the game's logic. Also, as mentioned earlier, the `pygame.event.get()` function gets the type of event; according to what is pressed, it changes the state of some parameters. For example, pressing the *Esc* key causes the game to quit, and pressing the arrow keys changes the direction of the snake. After that, we check whether the new direction is directly opposite to the old direction and change the direction only if it isn't. In this case, `changedDir` is only an intermediate variable. We then change the position of the snake according to the direction that's selected. Each shift in position signifies a shift of 20 pixels on screen:

```
snakeSeg.insert(0,list(snakePos))
if snakePos[0] == foodPosition[0] and snakePos[1] == foodPosition[1]:
foodSpawned = 0
Score = Score + 1
SpeedCount = SpeedCount + 1
```

```
if SpeedCount == 5 :
SpeedCount = 0
Speed = Speed + 1
else:
snakeSeg.pop()

if foodSpawned == 0:
x = random.randrange(1,40)
y = random.randrange(1,30)
foodPosition = [int(x*20),int(y*20)]
foodSpawned = 1

gameSurface.fill(backgroundcolor)
for position in snakeSeg:
pygame.draw.rect(gameSurface,snakecolor,Rect(position[0], position[1],
20, 20))
pygame.draw.circle(gameSurface,foodcolor,(foodPosition[0]+10,
foodPosition[1]+10), 10, 0)
pygame.display.flip()
if snakePos[0] > 780 or snakePos[0] < 0:
finish()
if snakePos[1] > 580 or snakePos[1] < 0:
finish()
for snakeBody in snakeSeg[1:]:
if snakePos[0] == snakeBody[0] and snakePos[1] == snakeBody[1]:
finish()
fpsClock.tick(Speed)
```

It is important to keep in mind that at this point, nothing is rendered on screen. We are just implementing the logic for the game, and only after we are done with that will anything be rendered on the screen. This will be done with the pygame. display.flip() function. Another important thing is that there is another function named pygame.display.update(). The difference between these two is that the update() function only updates specific areas of the surface, whereas the flip() function updates the entire surface. However, if we don't give any arguments to the update() function, then it will also update the entire surface.

Now, since we changed the position of the head of the snake, we have to update the `snakeSeg` variable to reflect this change in the snake body. For this, we use the `insert()` method and give the position of object we want to append and the new coordinates. This adds the new coordinates of the snake head into the `snakeSeg` variable. Then comes the interesting part, where we check whether the snake has reached the food. If it has, we increment the score, set the `foodSpawned` state to `False`, and increase `SpeedCount` by one. So, once the speed count reaches five, the speed is increased by one unit. If not, then we remove the last coordinate with the `pop()` method. This is interesting because if the snake has eaten the food, then its length will increase; consequently, the `pop()` method in the `else` statement will not be executed, and the length of the snake will be increased by one unit.

In the next block of code, we check whether the food is spawned; if not, we randomly spawn it, keeping in mind the dimensions of the screen. The `randrange()` function from the random package allows us to do exactly that.

Finally, we get to the part where the actual rendering takes place. Rendering is nothing but a term for the process that is required to generate and display something on screen. The first statement fills the screen with our selected background color so that everything else on the screen is easily visible:

```
for position in snakeSeg:
    pygame.draw.rect(gameSurface,snakecolor,Rect(position[0], position[1],
    20, 20))
```

The preceding block of code loops through all the coordinates present in the `snakeSeg` variable and fills the space between them with the color specified for our snake in the initialization code. The `rect` function takes three inputs: the window name on which the game will be played, the color of the rectangle, and the coordinates of the rectangle that are given by the `Rect` function. The `Rect` function itself takes four arguments: the `x` and `y` position and `height` and `width` of the rectangle. This means that for every coordinate contained in the `snakeSeg` variable, we draw on a rectangle that has dimensions of `20 x 20` pixels. So, we can see that we do not have to keep track of the snake as a whole; we only have to keep track of the coordinates that describe the snake.

Next, we draw our food using the `circle()` method from the `draw` module in the PyGame package. This method takes five arguments: the `window name`, the `color`, the `centre` of the circle, the `radius`, and the `width` of the circle. The centre of the circle is given by a tuple that contains the `x` and `y` coordinates that we selected previously. The next statement, `pygame.display.flip()`, actually displays what we have just drawn.

Then, we check for the conditions in which the game can end: hitting the wall or itself. When it hits an exit condition, the `finish()` function is called. The first two lines of the function are self-explanatory. In the third line, `render()` basically makes the text displayable. But it is not displayed yet. It will only be displayed once we call the `pygame.display.flip()` function. The next two lines set the position of the textbox that will be displayed on the window. And, finally, we quit the PyGame window and the program after a delay of 5 seconds.

Save this program in a file named `prog2.py` and run it using the following command:

`python prog2.py`

This is what you will be greeted with:

We can play the game for as long as we want (and we should because it's our creation) and when we exit, the game will be greeted by the same message that was defined in the `finish()` function!

As you may recognize, in the preceding screenshot, the black shape is the snake and the green circle is its food. You can play around with it and try to get an idea of the logic behind this game as to how it might be programmed.

With this, we complete the implementation of the snake game, and you should try out the program for yourself. An even better way to fully understand how the program works is to change some parameters and see how that affects the playing experience.

Summary

In this chapter, we learned about PyGame and its capabilities. We also learned how to build a binary fractal tree with random branches.

Furthermore, we built a snake game and used it to gain further experience in programming games using PyGame. You can also modify the game to gain any additional features you like.

Using these examples as an inspiration, you can also try to build games of your own. You can combine your knowledge of the chapter on Minecraft to build your own simple Minecraft clone!

In the next chapter, we will learn about the basics of Pi Camera and its webcam and how to capture images using them. We will also build some real-life examples using the Python language.

Working with a Webcam and Pi Camera

In the previous chapter, we learned how to set up and write our own games using pygame. In this chapter, we will learn how to use different types and uses of cameras with our Pi. Let's take a look at the topics we will study and implement in this chapter:

- Working with a webcam
- Crontab
- Timelapse using a webcam
- Webcam video recording and playback
- Pi Camera and Pi NoIR comparison
- Timelapse using Pi Camera
- The PiCamera module in Python

Working with webcams

USB webcams are a great way to capture images and videos. Raspberry Pi supports common USB webcams.

 To be on the safe side, here is a list of the webcams supported by Pi: http://elinux.org/RPi_USB_Webcams.

I am using a Logitech HD c310 USB Webcam as shown in the following image:

 You can purchase it online, and you can find the product details and the specifications at http://www.logitech.com/en-in/product/hd-webcam-c310.

Attach your USB webcam to Raspberry Pi through the USB port on Pi and run the **lsusb** command in the terminal. This command lists all the USB devices connected to the computer. The output should be similar to the following output depending on which port is used to connect the USB webcam:

```
pi@raspberrypi ~/book/chapter04 $ lsusb
Bus 001 Device 002: ID 0424:9514 Standard Microsystems Corp.
Bus 001 Device 001: ID 1d6b:0002 Linux Foundation 2.0 root hub
Bus 001 Device 003: ID 0424:ec00 Standard Microsystems Corp.
Bus 001 Device 004: ID 148f:2070 Ralink Technology, Corp. RT2070 Wireless
Adapter
Bus 001 Device 007: ID 046d:081b Logitech, Inc. Webcam C310
Bus 001 Device 006: ID 1c4f:0003 SiGma Micro HID controller
Bus 001 Device 005: ID 1c4f:0002 SiGma Micro Keyboard TRACER Gamma Ivory
```

Then, install the **fswebcam** utility by running the following command:

```
sudo apt-get install fswebcam
```

fswebcam is a simple command-line utility that captures images with webcams for Linux computers. Once the installation is done, you can use the following command to create a directory for output images:

```
mkdir /home/pi/book/output
```

Then, run the following command to capture the image:

```
fswebcam -r 1280x960 --no-banner ~/book/output/camtest.jpg
```

This will capture an image with a resolution of 1280 x 960. You might want to try another resolution for your learning. The **--no-banner** command will disable the timestamp banner. The image will be saved with the filename mentioned. If you run this command multiple times with the same filename, the image file will be overwritten each time. So, make sure that you change the filename if you want to save previously captured images. The text output of the command should be similar to the following output:

```
--- Opening /dev/video0...
Trying source module v4l2...
/dev/video0 opened.
No input was specified, using the first.
--- Capturing frame...
Corrupt JPEG data: 2 extraneous bytes before marker 0xd5
Captured frame in 0.00 seconds.
--- Processing captured image...
Disabling banner.
Writing JPEG image to '/home/pi/book/output/camtest.jpg'.
```

Crontab

Cron is a time-based job scheduler in Unix-like computer operating systems. It is driven by a **crontab** (cron table) file, which is a configuration file that specifies shell commands to be run periodically on a given schedule. It is used to schedule commands or shell scripts to run periodically at a fixed time, date, or interval.

The syntax for **crontab** in order to schedule a command or script is as follows:

```
1 2 3 4 5 /location/command
```

Here are the definitions:

- 1: Minutes (0-59)
- 2: Hours (0-23)
- 3: Days (0-31)
- 4: Months [0-12 (1 for January)]
- 5: Days of the week [0-7 (7 or 0 for Sunday)]
- `/location/command`: The script or command name to be scheduled

The `crontab` entry to run any script or command every minute is as follows:

```
* * * * * /location/command 2>&1
```

We will be using `crontab` in many chapters in this book. In the next section, we will learn how to use `crontab` to schedule a script to capture images periodically in order to create the timelapse sequence.

 You can refer to this URL for more details on `crontab`: `http://www.adminschoice.com/crontab-quick-reference`.

Creating a timelapse sequence using fswebcam

Timelapse photography means capturing photographs in regular intervals and playing the images with a higher frequency in time than those that were shot. For example, if you capture images with a frequency of one image per minute for 10 hours, you will get 600 images. If you combine all these images in a video with 30 images per second, you will get 10 hours of timelapse video compressed in 20 seconds. You can use your USB webcam with Raspberry Pi to achieve this. We already know how to use the Raspberry Pi with a webcam and the fswebcam utility to capture an image. The trick is to write a script that captures images with different names and then add this script in `crontab` and make it run at regular intervals.

Begin with creating a directory for captured images:

```
mkdir /home/pi/book/output/timelapse
```

Open an editor of your choice, write the following code, and save it as
timelapse.sh:

```
#!/bin/bash

DATE=$(date +"%Y-%m-%d_%H%M")
fswebcam -r 1280x960 --no-banner
/home/pi/book/output/timelapse/garden_$DATE.jpg
```

Make the script executable using:

```
chmod +x timelapse.sh
```

This shell script captures the image and saves it with the current timestamp in its
name. Thus, we get an image with a new filename every time as the file contains
the timestamp. The second line in the script creates the timestamp that we're
using in the filename. Run this script manually once, and make sure that the
image is saved in the **/home/pi/book/output/timelapse** directory with the
garden_<timestamp>.jpg name.

To run this script at regular intervals, we need to schedule it in **crontab**.

The **crontab** entry to run our script every minute is as follows:

```
* * * * * /home/pi/book/chapter04/timelapse.sh 2>&1
```

Open the **crontab** of the Pi user with **crontab -e**. It will open **crontab** with
nano as the editor. Add the preceding line to **crontab**, save it, and exit it.

Once you exit **crontab**, it will show the following message:

```
no crontab for pi - using an empty one

crontab: installing new crontab
```

Our timelapse webcam setup is now live. If you want to change the image capture
frequency, then you have to change the crontab settings. To set it every 5 minutes,
change it to ***/5 * * * ***. To set it for every 2 hours, use **0 */2 * * ***. Make
sure that your MicroSD card has enough free space to store all the images for the
time duration for which you need to keep your timelapse setup.

Once you capture all the images, the next part is to encode them all in a fast playing video, preferably 20 to 30 frames per second. For this part, the **mencoder** utility is recommended. The following are the steps to create a timelapse video with **mencoder** on a Raspberry Pi or any Debian/Ubuntu machine:

1. Install **mencoder** using `sudo apt-get install mencoder`

2. Navigate to the output directory by using:

   `cd /home/pi/book/output/timelapse`

3. Create a list of your timelapse sequence images using:

   `ls garden_*.jpg > timelapse.txt`

4. Use the following command to create a video:

   ```
   mencoder -nosound -ovc lavc -lavcopts vcodec=mpeg4:aspect=16
   /9:vbitrate=8000000 -vf scale=1280:960 -o timelapse.avi -mf
   type=jpeg:fps=30 mf://@timelapse.txt
   ```

This will create a video with name `timelapse.avi` in the current directory with all the images listed in `timelapse.txt` with a 30 fps frame rate. The statement contains the details of the video codec, aspect ratio, bit rate, and scale. For more information, you can run **man mencoder** on Command Prompt. We will cover how to play a video in the next section.

Webcam video recording and playback

We can use a webcam to record live videos using **avconv**. Install **avconv** using `sudo apt-get install libav-tools`. Use the following command to record a video:

```
avconv -f video4linux2 -r 25 -s 1280x960 -i /dev/video0 ~/book/output/
VideoStream.avi
```

It will show following output on the screen:

```
pi@raspberrypi ~ $ avconv -f video4linux2 -r 25 -s 1280x960 -i /dev/
video0 ~/book/output/VideoStream.avi
avconv version 9.14-6:9.14-1rpi1rpi1, Copyright (c) 2000-2014 the Libav
developers
  built on Jul 22 2014 15:08:12 with gcc 4.6 (Debian 4.6.3-14+rpi1)
[video4linux2 @ 0x5d6720] The driver changed the time per frame from 1/25
to 2/15
[video4linux2 @ 0x5d6720] Estimating duration from bitrate, this may be
inaccurate
```

```
Input #0, video4linux2, from '/dev/video0':
  Duration: N/A, start: 629.030244, bitrate: 147456 kb/s
    Stream #0.0: Video: rawvideo, yuyv422, 1280x960, 147456 kb/s, 1000k
tbn, 7.50 tbc
Output #0, avi, to '/home/pi/book/output/VideoStream.avi':
  Metadata:
    ISFT            : Lavf54.20.4
    Stream #0.0: Video: mpeg4, yuv420p, 1280x960, q=2-31, 200 kb/s, 25
tbn, 25 tbc
Stream mapping:
  Stream #0:0 -> #0:0 (rawvideo -> mpeg4)
Press ctrl-c to stop encoding
frame=  182 fps=  7 q=31.0 Lsize=     802kB time=7.28 bitrate=
902.4kbits/s
video:792kB audio:0kB global headers:0kB muxing overhead 1.249878%
Received signal 2: terminating.
```

You can terminate the recording sequence by pressing *Ctrl + C*.

We can play the video using **omxplayer**. It comes with the latest raspbian, so there is no need to install it. To play a file with the name **vid.mjpg**, use the following command:

```
omxplayer ~/book/output/VideoStream.avi
```

It will play the video and display some output similar to the one here:

```
pi@raspberrypi ~ $ omxplayer ~/book/output/VideoStream.avi
Video codec omx-mpeg4 width 1280 height 960 profile 0 fps 25.000000
Subtitle count: 0, state: off, index: 1, delay: 0
V:PortSettingsChanged: 1280x960@25.00 interlace:0 deinterlace:0
anaglyph:0 par:1.00 layer:0
have a nice day ;)
```

Try playing timelapse and record videos using **omxplayer**.

Working with the Pi Camera and NoIR Camera modules

These camera modules are specially manufactured for Raspberry Pi and work with all the available models. You will need to connect the camera module to the CSI port, located behind the Ethernet port, and activate the camera using the `raspi-config` utility if you haven't already.

 You can find the video instructions to connect the camera module to Raspberry Pi at http://www.raspberrypi.org/help/camera-module-setup/.

This page lists the types of camera modules available: http://www.raspberrypi.org/products/.

Two types of camera modules are available for the Pi. These are Pi Camera and Pi NoIR camera, and they can be found at https://www.raspberrypi.org/products/camera-module/ and https://www.raspberrypi.org/products/pi-noir-camera/, respectively.

The following image shows Pi Camera and Pi NoIR Camera boards side by side:

The following image shows the Pi Camera board connected to the Pi:

The following is an image of the Pi Camera board placed in the camera case:

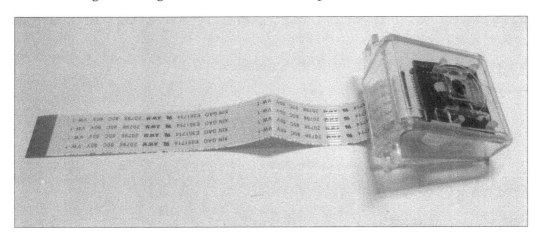

The main difference between Pi Camera and Pi NoIR Camera is that Pi Camera gives better results in good lighting conditions, whereas Pi NoIR (NoIR stands for No-Infra Red) is used for low light photography. To use NoIR Camera in complete darkness, we need to flood the object to be photographed with infrared light.

 This is a good time to take a look at the various enclosures for Raspberry Pi Models. You can find various cases available online at https://www.adafruit.com/categories/289.

An example of a Raspberry Pi case is as follows:

Using raspistill and raspivid

To capture images and videos using the Raspberry Pi Camera module, we need to use raspistill and raspivid utilities.

To capture an image, run the following command:

```
raspistill -o cam_module_pic.jpg
```

This will capture and save the image with name **cam_module_pic.jpg** in the current directory.

To capture a 20 second video with the camera module, run the following command:

```
raspivid -o test.avi -t 20000
```

This will capture and save the video with name **test.avi** in the current directory. Unlike **fswebcam** and **avconv**, **raspistill** and **raspivid** do not write anything to the console. So, you need to check the current directory for the output. Also, one can run the **echo $?** command to check whether these commands executed successfully. We can also mention the complete location of the file to be saved in these command, as shown in the following example:

```
raspistill -o /home/pi/book/output/cam_module_pic.jpg
```

Just like **fswebcam**, **raspistill** can be used to record the timelapse sequence. In our timelapse shell script, replace the line that contains **fswebcam** with the appropriate **raspistill** command to capture the timelapse sequence and use **mencoder** again to create the video. This is left as an exercise for the readers.

Now, let's take a look at the images taken with the Pi Camera under different lighting conditions.

The following is the image with normal lighting and the backlight:

The following is the image with only the backlight:

The following is the image with normal lighting and no backlight:

For NoIR camera usage in the night under low light conditions, use IR illuminator light for better results. You can get it online. A typical off-the-shelf LED IR illuminator suitable for our purpose will look like the one shown here:

Using picamera in Python with the Pi Camera module

The **picamera** is a Python package that provides a programming interface to the Pi Camera module. The most recent version of raspbian has `picamera` preinstalled. If you do not have it installed, you can install it using:

```
sudo apt-get install python-picamera
```

The following program quickly demonstrates the basic usage of the `picamera` module to capture an image:

```
import picamera
import time

with picamera.PiCamera() as cam:
    cam.resolution=(1024,768)
    cam.start_preview()
    time.sleep(5)
    cam.capture('/home/pi/book/output/still.jpg')
```

We have to import time and `picamera` modules first. **cam.start_preview()** will start the preview, and **time.sleep(5)** will wait for 5 seconds before **cam.capture()** captures and saves image in the specified file.

There is a built-in function in **picamera** for timelapse photography. The following program demonstrates its usage:

```
import picamera
import time

with picamera.PiCamera() as cam:
    cam.resolution=(1024,768)
    cam.start_preview()
    time.sleep(3)
    for count,
    imagefile in enumerate(cam.capture_continuous
    ('/home/pi/book/output/image{counter:
    02d}.jpg')):
        print 'Capturing and saving ' + imagefile
        time.sleep(1)
        if count == 10:
            break
```

In the preceding code, `cam.capture_continuous()` is used to capture the timelapse sequence using the Pi camera module.

> Checkout more examples and API references for the picamera module at http://picamera.readthedocs.org/.

The Pi camera versus the webcam

Now, after using the webcam and the Pi Camera, it's a good time to understand the differences, the pros, and the cons of using these.

The Pi camera board does not use a USB port and is directly interfaced to the Pi. So, it provides better performance than a webcam in terms of the frame rate and resolution. We can directly use the **picamera** module in Python to work on images and videos. However, the Pi camera cannot be used with any other computer.

A webcam uses an USB port for interface, and because of that, it can be used with any computer. However, compared to the Pi Camera its performance, it is lower in terms of the frame rate and resolution.

Summary

In this chapter, we learned how to use a webcam and the Pi camera. We also learned how to use utilities such as **fswebcam**, **avconv**, **raspistill**, **raspivid**, mencoder, and omxplayer. We covered how to use **crontab**. We used the Python **picamera** module to programmatically work with the Pi camera board. Finally, we compared the Pi camera and the webcam. We will be reusing all the code examples and concepts for some real-life projects soon.

In the next chapter, we will learn about programming Pi GPIO with PiGlow, which is a third-party add-on board for the Pi.

5
Introduction to GPIO Programming

In the previous chapter, we learned how to use a webcam and Pi Camera to capture images and videos. We also built a timelapse photography box to get experience about the real-life uses of what we learned.

In this chapter, we are going to adopt a hardware-focused approach and use Raspberry Pi's most talked about feature: its **GPIO** (short for **General Purpose Input Output**) pins. Specifically, we will learn how to use GPIO pins on Raspberry Pi B+ and Raspberry Pi 2. Once we get familiar with the use of the pins, we will also build a real-life project to further our knowledge of their use. The following topics will be covered in the chapter:

- Introducing GPIO pins
- Blinking an LED with GPIO pins
- Adding push button controls
- Learning about PiGlow

Introducing GPIO pins

Most of you may know where GPIO pins are located on the Raspberry Pi. If not, the following illustration will make it clear:

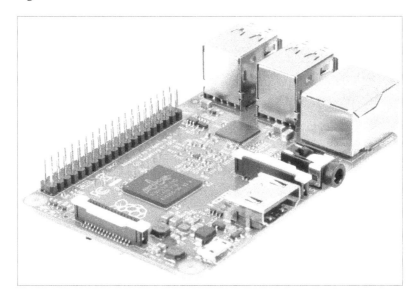

The following is a top view of the Raspberry Pi B+ board, which will help you see the components even more clearly:

The following diagram of the GPIO pins gives information about the naming convention and the function of each of the pins:

 Note that the GPIO pins of Raspberry Pi B+ and Pi 2 are the same.

Raspberry Pi B+ and Pi 2 J8 Header

Pin#	NAME			NAME	Pin#
01	3.3v DC Power			DC Power 5v	02
03	GPIO2 (SDA1 , I2C)			DC Power 5v	04
05	GPIO3 (SCL1 , I2C)			Ground	06
07	GPIO4 (GPIO_GCLK)			(TXD0) GPIO14	08
09	Ground			(RXD0) GPIO15	10
11	GPIO17 (GPIO_GEN0)			(GPIO_GEN1) GPIO18	12
13	GPIO27 (GPIO_GEN2)			Ground	14
15	GPIO22 (GPIO_GEN3)			(GPIO_GEN4) GPIO23	16
17	3.3v DC Power			(GPIO_GEN5) GPIO24	18
19	GPIO10 (SPI_MOSI)			Ground	20
21	GPIO9 (SPI_MISO)			(GPIO_GEN6) GPIO25	22
23	GPIO11 (SPI_CLK)			(SPI_CE0_N) GPIO8	24
25	Ground			(SPI_CE1_N) GPIO7	26
27	ID_SD (I2C ID EEPROM)			(I2C ID EEPROM) ID_SC	28
29	GPIO5			Ground	30
31	GPIO6			GPIO12	32
33	GPIO13			Ground	34
35	GPIO19			GPIO16	36
37	GPIO26			GPIO20	38
39	Ground			GPIO21	40

As you can see from the preceding diagram, there are four power pins, two for 3.3V and two for 5V, 8 ground pins distributed across the rail, 26 GPIO pins—some of which also provide protocols such as UART, SPI, PCM, PWM, I2C—and two pins reserved for accessing the EEPROM via I2C.

GPIO pins can be ON or OFF and HIGH or LOW. When a 3.3V pin is high, it outputs 3.3V, and when it is low, it outputs 0V. A GPIO pin can act as an input as well as an output but not both at the same time. To use it as an output is as simple as setting the pin state to ON or OFF.

To use GPIO pins, we will use a simple Python library called RPi.GPIO, which takes out all the effort and makes it easy to configure and use the pins. Configuring a pin to be an output or an input requires only a single statement. We will now see how to manipulate GPIO pins to use this library.

Take care to use Broadcom chip names for the GPIO pins. You can look this up in the diagram given earlier. If our pin has been set to the output mode, we can also set its activation or voltage level to HIGH or LOW. Keep in mind that in the case of the Raspberry Pi, high voltage is represented by 3.3V, and low voltage is represented by 0V. It will be damaging for the Raspberry Pi if you connect a 5V device to its 3.3V GPIO pins. However, you can use two 5V pins to power a small add-on, such as an LED or a buzzer. If you plan to use anything that requires more current, ensure that you use a separate power supply as the Pi can supply only a limited current. So, directly powering a motor from the Pi is not a good idea.

You can do amazing things with the input pins. Not only can you take inputs from a button, but you can also connect sensors, such as a light sensor, smoke sensor, and temperature sensor to build all kinds of amazing projects. You can also use an Internet-connected Raspberry Pi to control your outputs from anywhere in the world! But the networking part is outside the scope of this chapter.

A simple project at this point would be to build a simple LED blinking program. So let's see how that works!

Building an LED Blinker

For this project, you will require a humble low-power LED with the color of your choice, which can be obtained at your local hardware store or can be ordered online. The Raspberry Pi will act as both the switch and the power supply. In fact, we will power and switch the LED from the same output pin. The complete code and the wiring diagram has been given here. We will learn the code line by line following the diagram. Connect your LED to the Raspberry Pi, as shown. In an LED, the longer leg is the positive pin by convention, and the shorter leg has negative polarity. So take care to connect it the right way, or it might get damaged:

```
import RPi.GPIO as GPIO
import time

GPIO.setmode(GPIO.BOARD)
GPIO.setup(7, GPIO.OUT)

def Blink(speed):
    GPIO.output(7,True)
    time.sleep(speed)
```

```
GPIO.output(7,False)
time.sleep(speed)
GPIO.cleanup()
```

```
Blink(1)
```

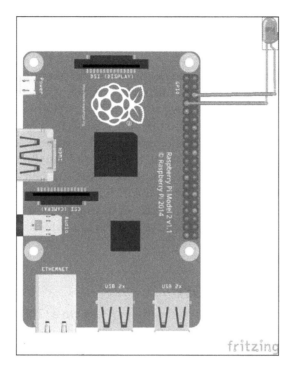

Once you've connected the LED as shown, go ahead and save the code as `prog1.py`, and execute the following command:

python prog1.py

If everything goes according to the plan, you should now see your LED blinking. Now we will analyze the code to see what exactly was done.

As usual, we begin the Python program by importing the required dependencies. `RPi.GPIO` is the Python library that provides the API that allows us to use GPIO pins. It is preinstalled on the Raspbian operating system. Then, we import the time module that will provide us with the delay for the blink.

`GPIO.setmode()` sets the addressing mode of the GPIO pins. There are two modes, namely BOARD and BCM. The BOARD mode addresses the pins by the numbering given on the board. For example, in the preceding GPIO diagram, the GPIO04 is pin 7. The other mode is BCM and it defines the pins according to the Broadcom Firmware on the Raspberry Pi. So, the GPIO04 pin will be referred to as 4 rather than 7. The next statement, `GPIO.setup()`, configures the specified pin to be an output or input depending on the argument.

Now, we'll move on to the main chunk of the code, which is the `Blink()` function. The `GPIO.output()` function takes two arguments: the pin number and the logical operation to be performed. In the first output statement, we set pin 7 to HIGH, and then in the second output statement, we set it to LOW. In between these functions, we have the `sleep()` function from the time package, which takes only one argument: the time in seconds. It does nothing but delay the execution of the next statement by the input number of seconds, which could also be fractions such as 0.5 or 0.2. The last statement in the `Blink()` function is the `cleanup()` function, which resets all the ports you have used back to the input mode. This prevents the pin from being damaged when you have set HIGH as an output and then accidentally connect it to ground, which would short-circuit the port. So, it's safer to leave the ports as inputs.

Connecting a button

As we saw in the previous section, connecting an LED to a GPIO pin was easy, and the code was simple. In this section, we will use the same general code in order to program a GPIO pin to take an input from the button and if the button is pressed, light the LED that we have already connected in the previous section. We will now take a look at the code and then explain those lines that were not encountered in the previous section:

```
import RPi.GPIO as GPIO
import time

GPIO.setmode(GPIO.BOARD)

GPIO.setup(12, GPIO.IN, pull_up_down = GPIO.PUD_UP)
GPIO.setup(7, GPIO.OUT)

while True:
    input_state = GPIO.input(12)

if input_state == False:
    print('Button Pressed')
GPIO.output(7, True)
```

```
else :
    print('Button Not Pressed')
GPIO.output(7, False)
```

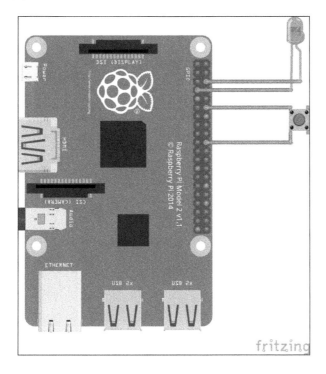

Now, save the code as prog2.py and run it with the following command:

python prog2.py

In this section, we configure pin #12 (by board numbering) to be an output via the same GPIO.setup() statement that we used in the previous section. But here, we have an extra argument, pull_up_down=GPIO.PUD_UP. This means that the internal resistor for the GPIO pin is being pulled up to 3.3V, and it will return False when the button is pressed. This is a little counter-intuitive, but without pulling up or down, the input will be left "floating", which means that the Pi will not be able to determine a button press simply because it does not have anything to compare the voltage level to!

Now we enter the infinite while loop, where it checks for the button state using the GPIO.input() function. As mentioned earlier, if the button is pressed, input_state will return False and the LED will be lit up. If, instead, the button is not pressed anymore, the LED will go off!

Simple, isn't it? Let's move on a more complicated add-on.

Installing PiGlow

The following figure shows the PiGlow board:

Since we have learned how to control an LED and a button via Raspberry Pi GPIO pins, we will now move on to a module called PiGlow, which is an add-on board for the Raspberry Pi and provides 18 individually controlled LEDs, and which you can use via a provided library. We will now proceed to install the software requirements for PiGlow by using a script provided by Pimoroni itself. To install PiGlow, run the following command in a new terminal:

```
curl get.pimoroni.com/piglow | bash
```

To check whether PiGlow has been installed properly, open a Python terminal and execute the following command:

```
import piglow
```

If it is successful, then continue.

To confirm whether I2C has been enabled, open the Raspberry Pi configuration tool by entering the following command:

```
sudo raspi-config
```

Then, select the **Advanced Options** menu from the displayed options.

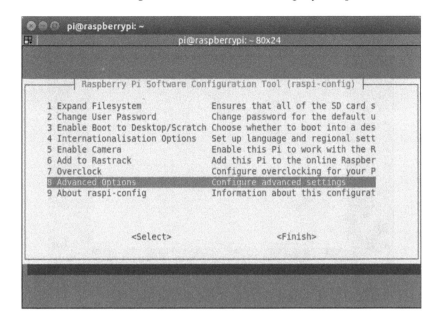

When we enter the **Advanced Options** menu of raspi-config, we are greeted by the following screen. We will now select the **A7** option, which is **I2C**.

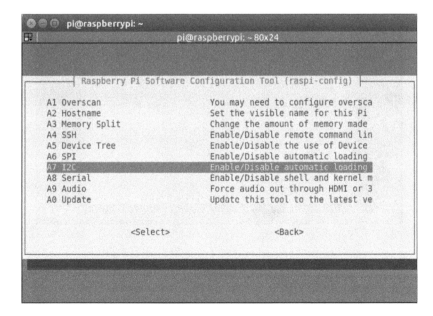

Once we select the **I2C** menu, the following display will be shown:

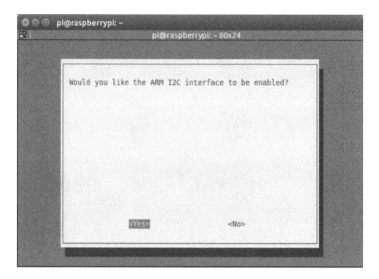

Select **Yes** for both the previous screen and the following one:

Using PiGlow

PiGlow has a set of female GPIO railings, which cover the Raspberry Pi's male GPIO rails. In case of Raspberry Pi 2 and B+, the size of the railing in PiGlow is shorter, so we need to make sure that PiGlow is attached to only lower numbered pins on the Raspberry Pi.

 You can find out more about PiGlow on the Pimoroni website at https://shop.pimoroni.com/products/piglow.

We can now proceed to control the LEDs on the PiGlow board. Open up a Python terminal and execute the following statements in a sequential order:

```
import piglow
piglow.red(64)
```

Here, we import the particular library in Python first. The `red()` method selects all the red LEDs on the PiGlow board. It takes only one argument, the intensity of the LEDs, which can be a number from 0 to 255. You can also try to pass the number 255 to the `red()` method to see how it affects the intensity of the LED. In this case, passing 0 would mean that the LED is off. But once we execute the earlier two statements, nothing will happen. We have to update the PiGlow with our changes by issuing the following command:

piglow.show()

Why? Because if we are setting up a pattern, lighting the LED costs time and resources. However, we can use the show method to draw the changes instantaneously. If you find this strange, you can turn this off by turning auto-update on with the following command:

piglow.auto_update = True

Similar to the `red()` method used earlier, we also have functions to control different colors, namely white, blue, green, yellow, and orange.

But maybe we want to control each arm of the light rather than all the lights of a single color. Well, we can do that with the `arm()` function! Take a look:

piglow.arm(0, 128)

The arm function takes two arguments. The first is the number of the arm, and second is the intensity from 0 to 255. For example, in the earlier statement, we set the LEDs of the first arm to an intensity of value 128, which is half of the full level of brightness. Suppose we want to control arbitrary LEDs according to what we specify. We're in luck! The `set()` function lets us control individual LEDs. It can be used in the following ways:

- `set(0, 255)`: This sets LED 0 to full brightness
- `set([1, 3, 5], 200)`: This sets LEDs 1, 3, and 5 to a 200 level of brightness
- `set(0, [255, 255, 255])`: This sets three LEDs starting at 0 index to full brightness

Now that we have learned the basics of using PiGlow, we will move on to building real-life examples with it. First, we will build a very simple example that looks like the arms of PiGlow are like cycle's spokes. Cool, right? The code is given here, and an explanation is as follows:

```
import time
import piglow

i = 0

while True:
    print(i)
piglow.all(0)
piglow.set(i % 18, [15, 31, 63, 127, 255, 127, 63, 31, 15])
piglow.show()
i += 1
time.sleep(0.1)
```

Now save the program as `prog1.py` and run it with the following command:

`python prog1.py`

As with every Python program, we first import the dependencies required, which in this case are the time library and the PiGlow library we just installed. Next, we set up the counter to keep track of which LED we want to light up and to execute the bulk of the program we enter into an infinite `while` loop. This `while` loop will continue lighting the LEDs until we kill the program.

First, we print the status of the counter, and then we execute the `all()` function, which will refresh all the LEDs and ensure that they are turned off at the beginning. We then use the third form of the `set()` function we saw earlier. This means that starting from the zeroth LED, we light up nine LEDs in an ascending and then descending fashion. The `i % 18` will give the remainder of i divided by 18 so that the index of the LED remains within the range of 0 to 18 at all times. Then, we actually show the pattern that we set in the earlier statement via the `show()` function. Finally, we increment the counter and add a delay of 100 milliseconds.

This pattern gets repeated for every LED, and when done in quick succession, it appears like the spokes are cycling.

This was a very basic example, and now we're ready to move on to a more complicated one, which involves building a binary clock. Let's begin!

Building a binary clock

In this example, we will be building a binary clock using the club PiGlow in which each hour, minute, and second is represented by the three arms of PiGlow. The numbers are displayed in the binary format. We will now look at the code and learn what each part does:

```
import piglow
from time import sleep
from datetime import datetime

piglow.auto_update = True

show12hr = 1
ledbrightness = 10

piglow.all(0)

hourcount = 0
currenthour = 0
```

Like the previous example, we import PiGlow and the time libraries, but we also import an additional library, `datetime`, which gives us the current time. Then, we set the auto-update parameter to true so that PiGlow updates as soon as we make a change to it rather than pushing all the changes at once. We will now set some customization parameters, namely selecting between a 12-hour format or a 24-hour format and the brightness of the LEDs. With that completed, we refresh the LED to the 0 level and set the hour counters. Now we are ready to move on the meat of the code:

```
while True:
    time = datetime.now().time()
print(str(time))
hour = time.hour
min = time.minute
sec = time.second

if show12hr == 1:
    if hour > 12:
    hour = hour - 12

if currenthour != hour:
    hourcount = hour
currenthour = hour

for x in range(6):
    piglow.led(13 + x, (hour & (1 << x)) * ledbrightness)

for x in range(6):
    piglow.led(7 + x, (min & (1 << x)) * ledbrightness)

for x in range(6):
    piglow.led(1 + x, (sec & (1 << x)) * ledbrightness)

if hourcount != 0:
    sleep(0.5)
piglow.white(ledbrightness)
sleep(0.5)
hourcount = hourcount - 1
else :
    sleep(0.1)
```

The main code logic is executed inside an infinite while loop so that the program never stops.

We can now proceed to learn what it is that makes the program *tick*. First, we must determine the current time, which is done by the `datetime.now().time()` method. Then, we store each of current hour, minute, and time in a separate variable to display them on separate arms. In the next `if` statement, we merely check whether we want to display the 12-hour format, and if we do, we subtract 12 from the current hour if it is greater than 12. So, something like 15 will be represented as 3. We have two variables named `currenthour` and `hourcount`, which serve to keep the correct hour displayed on the PiGlow arm by decrementing `hourcount` whenever an hour passes. This way, the hour is decreased, which is necessary if we are using the 12 hour mode. To understand the next statements, which are actually responsible for lighting up the LEDs, we need to understand the logic operators in Python. Some of these are given as follows:

Operation	Description
X and Y	Logical AND
X or Y	Logical OR
Not X	Logical NOT
X | Y	Bitwise OR
X ^ Y	Bitwise XOR
X & Y	Bitwise AND
X << Y	Bitwise Left Shift
X >> Y	Bitwise Right Shift

We are now greeted with a `for` loop. It has a very simple format as follows:

for (variable) in range(upper limit): The variable is a counter that starts from 0 and gets incremented after each iteration even though we don't explicitly do it. The upper limit, specified as the argument of the `range()` method, tells the `for` loop how many iterations are to be executed.

So, for x in range(6), we will set up x as a counter and the loop will be executed exactly six times. This is preferred since each arm has six LEDs, and each of them can be set without having six separate statements.

To understand what the following piece of code does, we will need to delve into the world of binary numbers and bitwise operations. You will also notice that in the argument of the `led()` function, we are doing a bitwise operation of the numbers. Why so? In the first iteration of the `for` loop, the value of x is 0, and the binary representation of 1 is 00000001. So, the bitwise shift operation will introduce no change. In the second iteration, however, the value of x will be 1. So, a 1-bit left shift will result in the binary number 00000010, which is the representation of integer 2. Similarly, the third iteration will result in 00000100, which is binary for 4. Now, there is also the bitwise AND operation on the variables holding the values of hours, minutes, and seconds. Consider, for example, that the current hour is 3 p.m. The binary representation will be 00000011. If we do a bitwise AND operation in the first iteration, we get 00000001. This is 1 and it is multiplied with the `ledbrightness` variable; we light up the 13 + 0 = 13th LED at a brightness of 10. This LED is the first LED of the arm that is represented by hours. Now, doing a bitwise AND in the second iteration, we have hour = 00000011 and 1 << x = 00000010. The result is 00000010, which is the integer 2. This means that the 14th LED will light with a brightness of 20. But in the third iteration, since 1 << x = 00000100, we get the integer 0 at the output, which means that the 15th LED will not light at all!

Applying the same logic if the time is 4 pm, the 13th LED will not light up, the 14th LED will not light up, but the 15th LED will light up with a brightness of 40. Going in the same direction, we now have an intuitive understanding of how the hours, minutes, and seconds of the binary clock are represented.

Finally, we design the program to flash all the white LEDs once the hour finishes. We also add 500-ms delays on both sides of the flash so that it doesn't appear too sudden. Then, we decrement the hour count and the whole program repeats with the updated time.

Now, save the code as `prog3.py` and run it with the following command:

```
python prog3.py
```

You will now be able to see the hours, minutes, and seconds represented as binary numbers on PiGlow!

Summary

This chapter was particularly interesting and hands-on because we learned how to manipulate hardware from software! This is exactly the reason why the Raspberry Pi and other boards with GPIO pins have become so popular. They allow you to control real-life hardware applications with software.

We can create potentially unlimited applications for the Pi just by changing the sensors connected to it and tweaking the code. We can build stuff such as home automation systems, security applications, wearable devices, and many more with just this small board! In this chapter, we had the humble beginnings of such projects where we first learned to blink an LED, which wasn't very impressive by itself. Then, we learned how to control that same LED with a button, which was a bit more fun.

Then, we learned about PiGlow and how to connect it to the Raspberry Pi. We learned the various API commands that are used to control the LEDs on PiGlow, and using these commands, we built a binary clock.

With these solid foundations, we then moved on to an even more complicated undertaking, which involved a little theory and a bit of clever programming in Python, which greatly reduced our effort.

In our next chapter, we will learn how to create animated movies. We will use a more software-based approach and make animations such as stop motion.

6

Creating Animated Movies
with Raspberry Pi

In the previous chapter, we learned how to use GPIO pins to control LEDs and get input from buttons. We also learned how to control the PiGlow module with its provided Python API. In *Chapter 4, Working with Webcam and Pi Camera*, we learned how to operate Pi Camera or a general webcam to capture images and videos. In this chapter, we will combine the two concepts and learn how to create stop-motion animation. In this chapter, we will learn about the following:

- Creating a stop-motion animation using a push button
- Examining the theory behind stop-motion
- Revisiting some GPIO concepts
- Using the ffmpeg library to render the shots into a video

Introducing stop-motion animation

A **stop-motion animation** is basically a video of sequenced images, such as those where an object is physically manipulated so that it appears to move on its own when the video is played. The position of the object is changed incrementally after each shot so that over a course of multiple frames, it appears as though the object is moving. A common subject for stop-motion animations is a clay object, such as a bird, animal, and so on.

Setting up the prerequisites

In addition to the Raspberry Pi, for this chapter we will require the following:

- Pi Camera
- Tactile push button
- Breadboard
- A few jumper cables

1. The tactile button can be purchased from your local hardware shop or online from sellers such as Adafruit. It might look something like the following:

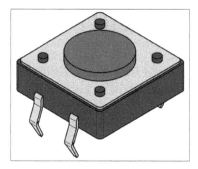

2. The breadboard is basically a temporary connection mechanism for electronic components. Each pin in the 5-pin row is connected to each other, so they behave as a common terminal for each component connected to the same row. All the pins in the side rail are electrically connected and primarily serve as power lines. A breadboard looks like the following:

Jumper cables are nothing but wires that allow us to connect different rows in a breadboard and look like this:

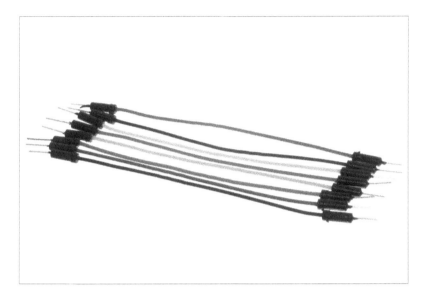

We will require the `ffmpeg` library installed on our Pi. This can be installed with the following command:

```
sudo apt-get install ffmpeg
```

Once the installation is finished, you can test it by executing the following command:

```
avconv
```

If it is installed properly, then you should see some information about the `avconv` tool. If not, then try to install it properly and then run the command again.

Setting up and testing the camera

Before booting up the Pi, we need to connect Pi Camera to it. This is as simple as locating the camera port beside the Ethernet port, inserting the camera strip in it, and pushing the tab down to secure it.

You can now test to check whether this works. After booting up the Pi, issue the following command:

```
raspistill -o image.jpg
```

If everything went fine, you should now see an image in your home directory. Open it to check whether the camera took a satisfactory picture. Don't worry if it is upside down as we will correct this shortly. It will look something like this:

Now, we will look at the code to take a picture with Python. As we did earlier, we will first see the code completely and then learn what it does statement by statement. Here it is:

```
import picamera
from time import sleep

with picamera.PiCamera() as camera:
    camera.start_preview()
    sleep(3)
    camera.capture('/home/pi/image.jpg')
    camera.stop_preview()
```

We first import the PI camera library, which is required to take pictures with PiCam. We also import the time library to provide delays in taking a picture. The next statement essentially ensures that we can access `picamera.PiCamera()` with the same camera. The `camera.start_preview()` method starts a preview screen for the camera, and after a delay of 3 seconds the `capture()` method takes a picture. The argument to the capture command gives the filename for the image file. Finally, the `stop_preview()` method stops the preview.

Save the file as `prog1.py` and run it with the following command as this is a `python3` program:

python3 prog1.py

Now, double-click on the new image file from the File Explorer and check whether it is upside down. If it is, then add the following two lines before the `start_preview()` method to correct it:

```
camera.vflip = True
camera.hflip = True
```

Adding the hardware button

To our current setup, we will add a hardware input button so that we can take pictures when we press that button. So, connect a tactile button to the Raspberry Pi, as shown in the following image:

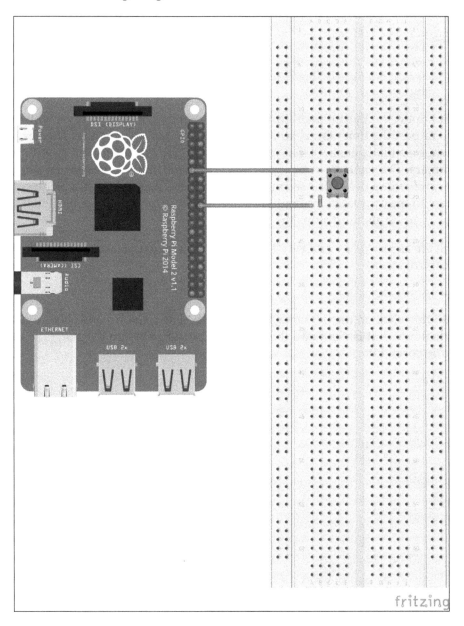

This time, we will use the BCM convention when specifying GPIO pins. We will connect the button to the GPIO17 pin. Then, we will modify the code so that it looks like the following:

```
import picamera
from RPi import GPIO

GPIO.setmode(GPIO.BCM)
GPIO.setup(17, GPIO.IN, GPIO.PUD_UP)

with picamera.PiCamera() as camera:
    camera.start_preview()
    GPIO.wait_for_edge(17, GPIO.FALLING)
    camera.capture('/home/pi/image.jpg')
    camera.stop_preview()
```

Save the preceding program as `prog2.py` and run it with the following command:

python3 prog2.py

We will now see what each line of code does, except those that we already saw in the previous program. To use the GPIO pins, we have to import the `RPi.GPIO` library, as we did in the previous chapter. Then, we set the GPIO addressing mode as BCM, which uses the Broadcom convention rather than numbering the pins on the board. This means that we can address the GPIO pin by its GPIO number rather than its board number. With the `setup()` method, we configure the pin to be an input and set it so that it is pulled up by default.

The function that actually does the magic is `wait_for_edge()`. It takes the pin number as the first argument and `GPIO_FALLING` as the second. This means that the function will be triggered only when the signal at pin 17 goes from high to low or when it falls. So, it will be triggered when the button goes from the pressed state to the unpressed state; that is, it will be triggered when we leave the button rather than when we press the button. The next statements capture and save the image and then exit the preview. If we want to take a selfie, then we can add a delay after the `wait_for_edge()` function in order to enable us to get into position. Also, don't forget to add the two commands to correct an upside down picture if such a need arises.

Now that we have successfully taken individual photos without a camera, it's time to try taking a series of still images and combining them in order to make a stop-motion animation. Just so that your home folder does not just get messy, we can create a new folder and enter it with the following commands:

mkdir stopmotion

cd stopmotion

Modify the given code and add a loop to take a picture every time the button is pressed. The new code looks like the following:

```
import picamera
from RPi import GPIO

GPIO.setmode(GPIO.BCM)
GPIO.setup(17, GPIO.IN, GPIO.PUD_UP)

with picamera.PiCamera() as camera:
    camera.start_preview()
    frame = 1
    while True:
        GPIO.wait_for_edge(17, GPIO.FALLING)
        camera.capture('/home/pi/stopmotion/frame%03d.jpg' % frame)
        frame += 1
    camera.stop_preview()
```

What we have done is create an infinite while loop that keeps taking photographs as long as the button is pressed. The frame variable keeps track of the current frame and saves the corresponding image in the folder.

 But be careful about the space limitations of your SD card. If we hold down the button for long, the Pi could run out of space and crash once it run out of space, causing us to lose all the data and potentially corrupting the SD card.

Now, save the program as `prog3.py` and run it with the following command:

python3 prog3.py

Run the program and collect as many images as required for our stop-motion project. Press *Ctrl + C* to exit the program and open the File Manager to see your images.

Rendering the video

We are now ready to render the video from the sequence of images we just collected. We will begin rendering the video by entering the terminal window. Navigate to the stopmotion folder with the following command:

cd /home/pi/stopmotion

Then, execute the following command to begin rendering the video:

avconv -r 10 -qscale 2 -i frame%03d.jpg animation.mp4

We will now see what each part of this command does:

- `-r` specifies the frame rate for the video, which is currently set at 10
- `-qscale` specifies the quality for the video and can range from 2-5
- `-i` specifies the input file

Once the rendering is complete, you can play it with the following command:

```
omxplayer animation.mp4
```

Congratulations! You have just created your own stop-motion animation creator! Go ahead and try it out. Build your own interesting animations and upload them on YouTube.

Summary

In this chapter, we revised how to use Pi Camera with the Raspberry Pi and take photos with it. We learned a neat trick to correct our photos if they are upside down. We also learned how to use a GPIO to use a tactile button to act as the trigger for our images.

Once we obtained the images required for our animation, we proceeded to combine those images in a video, where we specified the frame rate and quality. Finally, we rendered the video using the `ffmpeg` library.

In the next chapter, we will learn about the popular open source image processing library, OpenCV, and get it set up on the Raspberry Pi. We will also implement some interesting projects, such as video processing, logical operations on an image, colorspace conversions, and much more!

7
Introduction to Computer Vision

In the previous chapter, we implemented a battery-operated portable Pi time-lapse box and a stop motion recording system. In this chapter, we will cover the basics of computer vision with Pi using the OpenCV library. OpenCV is a simple yet powerful tool for any computer vision enthusiast. One can learn about computer vision in an easy way by writing OpenCV programs in Python. Using a Raspberry Pi computer and Python for OpenCV programming is one of the best ways to start your journey in the world of computer vision. We will cover the following topics in detail in this chapter:

- Introducing computer vision
- Introducing OpenCV
- Setting up Pi for computer vision and NumPy
- Image basics in OpenCV
- Webcam video processing with OpenCV
- Arithmetic and logical operations on images
- Colorspace and the conversion of colorspace
- Object tracking based on colors

Introducing Computer Vision

Computer vision is an area of computer science, mathematics, and electrical engineering. It includes ways to acquire, process, analyze, and understand images and videos from the real world in order to mimic human vision. Also, unlike human vision, computer vision can also be used to analyze and process depth and infrared images. Computer vision is also concerned with the theory of information extraction from images and videos. A computer vision system can accept different forms of data as an input, including — but not limited to — images, image sequences, and videos that can be streamed from multiple sources to further process and extract useful information from it for decision making. Artificial intelligence and computer vision share many topics, such as image processing, pattern recognition, and machine learning techniques.

Introducing OpenCV

OpenCV (short for **Open Source Computer Vision**) is a library of programming functions for computer vision. It was initially developed by the Intel Russia research center in Nizhny Novgorod, and it is currently maintained by Itseez.

You can read more about Itseez at http://itseez.com/.

This is a cross-platform library, which means that it can be implemented and operated on different operating systems. It focuses mainly on image and video processing. In addition to this, it has several GUI and event handling features for the user's convenience.

OpenCV was released under a **Berkeley Software Distribution** (**BSD**) license, and hence, it is free for both academic and commercial use. It has interfaces for popular programming languages, such as C/C++, Python, and Java, and it runs on a variety of operating systems, including Windows, Android, and Unix-like operating systems.

You can explore the OpenCV homepage, www.opencv.org, for further details.

OpenCV was initially an Intel Research initiative to develop tools to analyze images. The following is the timeline of OpenCV in brief:

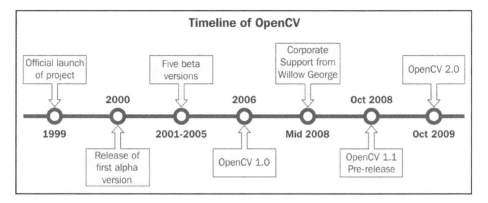

In August 2012, support for OpenCV was taken over by a nonprofit foundation, www.OpenCV.org, which is currently developing it further. It also maintains a developer and user site for OpenCV.

 At the time of writing this, the stable version of OpenCV is 2.4.10. Version 3.0 Beta is also available.

Setting up Pi for Computer Vision

Make sure that you have a working, wired Internet connection with reasonable speed for this activity. Now, let's prepare our Pi for computer vision:

1. Connect your Pi to the Internet through Ethernet or a Wi-Fi USB dongle.

2. Run the following command to restart the networking service:

```
sudo service networking restart
```

3. Make sure that Raspberry Pi is connected to the Internet by typing in the following command:

```
ping -c4 www.google.com
```

   If the command fails, then check the Internet connection with some other device and resolve the issue. After that, repeat the preceding steps again.

4. Run the following commands in a sequence:

```
sudo apt-get update
sudo apt-get upgrade
sudo rpi-update
sudo reboot -h now
```

5. After this, we will need to install a few necessary packages and dependencies for OpenCV. The following is the list of packages we need to install. You just need to connect your Pi to the Internet and type this in:

```
sudo apt-get install <package-name> -y
```

Here, `<package-name>` is one of the following packages:

libopencv-dev	libpng3	libdc1394-22-dev
build-essential	libpnglite-dev	libdc1394-22
libavformat-dev	zlib1g-dbg	libdc1394-utils
x264	zlib1g	libv4l-0
v4l-utils	zlib1g-dev	libv4l-dev
ffmpeg	pngtools	libpython2.6
libcv2.3	libtiff4-dev	python-dev
libcvaux2.3	libtiff4	python2.6-dev
libhighgui2.3	libtiffxx0c2	libgtk2.0-dev
libpng++-dev	libtiff-tools	libunicap2-dev
opencv-doc	libjpeg8	libeigen3-deva
libcv-dev	libjpeg8-dev	libswscale-dev
libcvaux-dev	libjpeg8-dbg	libjpeg-dev
libhighgui-dev	libavcodec-dev	libwebp-dev
python-numpy	libavcodec53	libpng-dev
python-scipy	libavformat53	libtiff5-dev
python-matplotlib	libgstreamer0.10-0-dbg	libjasper-dev
python-pandas	libgstreamer0.10-0	libopenexr-dev
python-nose	libgstreamer0.10-dev	libgdal-dev
v4l-utils	libxine1-ffmpeg	python-tk
libgtkglext1-dev	libxine-dev	python3-dev
libpng12-0	libxine1-bin	python3-tk
libpng12-dev	libunicap2	python3-numpy

For example, you have to install x264, then you will need to to type the following:

```
sudo apt-get install x264 -y
```

This will install the necessary package. Similarly, install all the previously mentioned packages. If a package is already installed on your Pi, then it will show the following message:

```
Reading package lists... Done
Building dependency tree
Reading state information... Done
x264 is already the newest version.
0 upgraded, 0 newly installed, 0 to remove and 0 not upgraded.
```

In this case, don't worry. This package is already installed and comes with its newest version. Just proceed with installing all the other packages in the list one by one.

6. Finally, install OpenCV for Python with this:

```
sudo apt-get install python-opencv -y
```

This is the easiest way to install OpenCV for Python; however, there is a problem with this. Raspbian repositories may not always contain the latest version of OpenCV. For example, at the time of writing this, Raspbian repository contains 2.4.1, while the latest OpenCV version is 2.4.10. With respect to the Python API, the latest version will always contain much better support and more functionality.

For the convenience of the readers, all these commands are included in an executable shell script, `chapter07.sh`, in the code bundle. Just run the script with the following command:

```
./chapter07.sh
```

This will install all the required packages and dependencies to get started with OpenCV on Pi.

Another method to do the same is to compile OpenCV from the source, which I will not recommend for beginners as it's a bit complex and will take a lot of time.

Testing the OpenCV installation with Python

In Python, it's very easy to code for OpenCV. It requires very few lines of code compared to C/C++, and powerful libraries such as NumPy can be exploited for multidimensional data structures required for image processing.

Open a terminal and type `python`, and then type the following lines:

```
>>> import cv2
>>> print cv2.__version__
```

This will show us the version of OpenCV installed on the Pi, which is 2.4.1 in our case.

Introducing NumPy

NumPy is the fundamental package used for scientific computing with Python and it is matrix library for linear algebra. NumPy can also be used as an efficient multidimensional container of generic data. Arbitrary datatypes can be defined and used. NumPy is an extension to the Python programming language, adding support for large, multidimensional arrays and matrices, along with a large library of high-level mathematical functions to operate on these arrays. We will be using NumPy arrays throughout this book in order to represent images and carry out complex mathematical operations on them. NumPy comes with many built-in functions for all these operations so that we do not have to worry about all the basic array operations. We can directly focus on the concepts and code for computer vision. All OpenCV array structures are converted to and from Numpy arrays. So, whatever operations you can compute in Numpy, we can process them with OpenCV.

In this book, we will be using NumPy with OpenCV a lot. Let's start with some simple example programs that will demonstrate the real power of NumPy.

Open `python` in the terminal and try out the upcoming examples.

Array creation

Let's look at some examples of array creation. `array()` method is used very frequently in the remainder of the book. There are many ways to create arrays of different types. We will explore these ways as and when required throughout the remainder of this book:

```
>>> import numpy as np
>>> x=np.array([1,2,3])
>>> x
array([1, 2, 3])


>>> y=range(10)
>>> y
array([0, 1, 2, 3, 4, 5, 6, 7, 8, 9])
```

Basic operations on arrays

We are going to learn about a `linspace()` function now. It takes three parameters: `start_num`, `end_num`, and `count`. This creates an array with equally spaced points starting with `start_num` and ending with `end_num`. Try out the following example:

```
>>> a=np.array([1,3,6,9])
>>> b=np.linspace(0,15,4)
>>> c=a-b
>>> c
array([ 1., -2., -4., -6.])
```

The following is the code to calculate the square of every element in an array:

```
>>> a**2
array([ 1,  9, 36, 81])
```

Linear algebra

Let's explore some linear algebra examples. We will look at the `transpose()`, `inv()`, `solve()`, and `dot()` functions, which are useful for linear algebra:

```
>>> a=np.array([[1,2,3],[4,5,6],[7,8,9]])
>>> a.transpose()
array([[1, 4, 7],
       [2, 5, 8],
       [3, 6, 9]])

>>> np.linalg.inv(a)
array([[ -4.50359963e+15,   9.00719925e+15,  -4.50359963e+15],
       [  9.00719925e+15,  -1.80143985e+16,   9.00719925e+15],
       [ -4.50359963e+15,   9.00719925e+15,  -4.50359963e+15]])

>>> b=np.array([3,2,1])
>>> np.linalg.solve(a,b)
array([ -9.66666667,  15.33333333,  -6.        ])

>>> c= np.random.rand(3,3)
>>> c
array([[ 0.69551123,  0.18417943,  0.0298238 ],
       [ 0.11574883,  0.39692914,  0.93640691],
       [ 0.36908272,  0.53802672,  0.2333465 ]])
>>> np.dot(a,c)
array([[ 2.03425705,  2.59211786,  2.60267713],
       [ 5.57528539,  5.94952371,  6.20140877],
       [ 9.11631372,  9.30692956,  9.80014041]])
```

 You can explore NumPy in detail at http://www.numpy.org/.

Working with images

Let's get started with the basics of OpenCV's Python API. All the scripts we will write and run will use the OpenCV library, which must be imported with the `import cv2` line. We will import few more libraries as required, and in the next sections and chapters, `cv2.imread()` will be used to import an image. It takes two arguments. The first argument is the image filename. The image should be in the same directory where the Python script is the absolute path that should be provided to `cv2.imread()`. It reads images and saves them as NumPy arrays.

The second argument is a flag that specifies that the mode image should be read. The flag can have the following values:

- `cv2.IMREAD_COLOR`: This loads a color image; it is the default flag
- `cv2.IMREAD_GRAYSCALE`: This loads an image in the grayscale mode
- `cv2.IMREAD_UNCHANGED`: This loads an image as it includes an alpha channel

The numeric values of the preceding flags are *1*, *0*, and *-1*, respectively.

Take a look at the following code:

```
import cv2 #This imports opencv
#This reads and stores image in color into variable img
img = cv2.imread('lena_color_512.tif',cv2.IMREAD_COLOR)
```

Now, the last line in the preceding code is the same as this:

```
img = cv2.imread('lena_color_512.tif',1)
```

We will be using the numeric values of this flag throughout the book.

The following code is used to display the image:

```
cv2.imshow('Lena',img)
cv2.waitKey(0)
cv2.destroyWindow('Lena')
```

The cv2.imshow() function is used to display an image. The first argument is a string that is the window name, and the second argument is the variable that holds the image that is to be displayed.

cv2.waitKey() is a keyboard function. Its argument is the time in milliseconds. The function waits for specified milliseconds for any keyboard key press. If 0 is passed, it waits indefinitely for a key press. It is the only method to fetch and handle events. We must use this for cv2.imshow() or no image will be displayed on screen.

cv2.destroyWindow() function takes a window name as a parameter and destroys that window. If we want to destroy all the windows in the current program, we can use cv2.destroyAllWindows().

We can also create a window with a specific name in advance and assign an image to that window later. In many cases, we will have to create a window before we have an image. This can be done using the following code:

```
cv2.namedWindow('Lena', cv2.WINDOW_AUTOSIZE)
cv2.imshow('Lena',img)
cv2.waitKey(0)
cv2.destroyAllWindows()
```

Putting it all together, we have the following script:

```
import cv2
img = cv2.imread('lena_color_512.tif',1)
cv2.imshow('Lena',img)
cv2.waitKey(0)
cv2.destroyWindow('Lena')
```

To summarize, the preceding script imports an image, displays it, and waits for the keystroke to close the window. The screenshot is as follows:

The cv2.imwrite() function is used to save an image to a specific path. The first argument is the name of the file and second is the variable pointing to the image we want to save. Also, cv2.waitKey() can be used to detect specific keystrokes. Let's test the usage of both the functions in the following code snippet:

```
import cv2
img = cv2.imread('lena_color_512.tif', 1)
cv2.imshow('Lena', img)
keyPress = cv2.waitKey(0)
if keyPress == ord('q'):
    cv2.destroyWindow('Lena')
elif keyPress == ord('s'): cv2.imwrite('output.jpg', img)
cv2.destroyWindow('Lena')
```

Here, keyPress = cv2.waitKey(0) is used to save the value of the keystroke in the keyPress variable. Given a string of length one, ord() returns an integer representing the Unicode code point of the character when the argument is a Unicode object or the value of the byte when the argument is an 8-bit string. Based on keyPress, we either exit or exit after saving the image. For example, if the *Esc* key is pressed, the cv2.waitKey() function will return *27*.

Using matplotlib

We can also use matplotlib to display images. matplotlib is a 2D plotting library for Python. It provides a wide range of plotting options, which we will be using in the next chapter. Let's look at a basic example of matplotlib:

```
import cv2
import matplotlib.pyplot as plt
#Program to load a color image in gray scale and to display using
  matplotlib
img = cv2.imread('lena_color_512.tif',0)
plt.imshow(img,cmap='gray')
plt.title('Lena')
plt.xticks([])
plt.yticks([])
plt.show()
```

In this example, we are reading an image in grayscale and displaying it using `matplotlib`. The following screenshot shows the plot of the image:

The `plt.xticks([])` and `plt.yticks([])` functions can be used to disable *x* and *y* axis. Run the preceding code again, and this time, comment out the two lines with the `plt.xticks([])` and `plt.yticks([])` functions.

The `cv2.imread()` OpenCV function reads images and saves them as NumPy arrays of Blue, Green, and Red (BGR) pixels.

However, `plt.imshow()` displays images in the RGB format. So, if we read an image as it is with `cv2.imread()` and display it using `plt.imshow()`, then the value for blue will be treated as the value for red and vice versa by `plt.imshow()`, and it will display an image with distorted colors. Try out the preceding code with the following alterations in the respective lines to experience the concept:

```
img = cv2.imread('lena_color_512.tif',1)
plt.imshow(img)
```

To remedy this issue, we need to convert an image read in the BGR format into an RGB array format by `cv2.imread()` so that `plt.imshow()` will be able to render it in a way that makes sense to us. We will be using the `cv2.cvtColor()` function for this, which we will learn soon.

[Explore this URL to get more information on `matplotlib`: `http://matplotlib.org/`.]

Working with Webcam using OpenCV

OpenCV has a functionality to work with standard USB webcams. Let's take a look at an example to capture an image from a webcam:

```
import cv2

# initialize the camera
cam = cv2.VideoCapture(0)
ret, image = cam.read()

if ret:
    cv2.imshow('SnapshotTest',image)
    cv2.waitKey(0)
    cv2.destroyWindow('SnapshotTest')
    cv2.imwrite('/home/pi/book/output/SnapshotTest.jpg',image)
cam.release()
```

In the preceding code, `cv2.VideoCapture()` creates a video capture object. The argument for it can either be a video device or a file. In this case, we are passing a device index, which is 0. If we have more cameras, then we can pass the appropriate device index based on what camera to choose. If you have one camera, just pass 0.

You can find out the number of cameras and associated device indexes using the following command:

```
ls -l /dev/video*
```

Once `cam.read()` returns a Boolean value `ret` and the `frame` which is the image it captured. If the image capture is successful, then `ret` will be *True*; otherwise, it will be False. The previously listed code will capture an image with the camera device, `/dev/video0`, display it, and then save it. `cam.release()` will release the device.

This code can be used with slight modifications to display live video stream from the webcam:

```
import cv2

cam = cv2.VideoCapture(0)
print 'Default Resolution is ' + str(int(cam.get(3))) + 'x' +
   str(int(cam.get(4)))
w=1024
h=768
cam.set(3,w)
cam.set(4,h)
print 'Now resolution is set to ' + str(w) + 'x' + str(h)

while(True):
    # Capture frame-by-frame
    ret, frame = cam.read()

    # Display the resulting frame
    cv2.imshow('Video Test',frame)

    # Wait for Escape Key
    if cv2.waitKey(1) == 27 :
        break

# When everything done, release the capture
cam.release()
cv2.destroyAllWindows()
```

You can access the features of the video device with `cam.get(propertyID)`. 3 stands for the width and 4 stands for the height. These properties can be set with `cam.set(propertyID, value)`.

The preceding code first displays the default resolution and then sets it to 1024 x 768 and displays the live video stream till the *Esc* key is pressed. This is the basic skeleton logic for all the live video processing with OpenCV. We will make use of this in future.

Saving a video using OpenCV

We need to use the `cv2.VideoWriter()` function to write a video to a file. Take a look at the following code:

```
import cv2
cam = cv2.VideoCapture(0)
output = cv2.VideoWriter('VideoStream.avi',
cv2.cv.CV_FOURCC(*'WMV2'),40.0,(640,480))

while (cam.isOpened()):
    ret, frame = cam.read()
    if ret == True:
        output.write(frame)
        cv2.imshow('VideoStream', frame )
        if cv2.waitKey(1) == 27 :
            break
    else:
        break

cam.release()
output.release()
cv2.destroyAllWindows()
```

In the preceding code, `cv2.VideoWriter()` accepts the following parameters:

- **Filename**: This is the name of the video file.
- **FourCC**: This stands for **Four Character Code**. We have to use the `cv2.cv.CV_FOURCC()` function for this. This function accepts FourCC in the *'code'* format. This means that for DIVX, we need to pass *'DIVX', and so on. Some supported formats are DIVX, XVID, H264, MJPG, WMV1, and WMV2.

 You can read more about FourCC at `www.fourcc.org`.

- **Framerate**: This is the rate of the frames to be captured per second.
- **Resolution**: This is the resolution of the video to be captured.

The preceding code records the video till the *Esc* key is pressed and saves it in the specified file.

Pi Camera and OpenCV

The following code demonstrates the use of Picamera with OpenCV. It shows a preview for 3 seconds, captures an image, and displays it on screen using `cv2.imshow()`:

```
import picamera
import picamera.array
import time
import cv2

with picamera.PiCamera() as camera:
    rawCap=picamera.array.PiRGBArray(camera)
    camera.start_preview()
    time.sleep(3)
    camera.capture(rawCap,format="bgr")
    image=rawCap.array
cv2.imshow("Test",image)
cv2.waitKey(0)
cv2.destroyAllWindows()
```

Retrieving image properties

We can retrieve and use many image properties with OpenCV functions. Take a look at the following code:

```
import cv2
img = cv2.imread('lena_color_512.tif',1)
print img.shape
print img.size
print img.dtype
```

The `img.shape` operation returns the shape of the image, that is, its dimensions and the number of color channels. The output of the previously listed code will be as follows:

```
(512, 512, 3)
786432
uint8
```

If the image is colored, then `img.shape` returns a triplet containing the number of rows, the number of columns, and the number of channels in the image. Usually, the number of channels is three, representing the red, green, and blue channels. If the image is grayscale, then `img.shape` only returns the number of rows and the number of columns. Try to modify the preceding code to read the image in the grayscale mode and observe the output of `img.shape`.

The `img.size` operation returns the total number of pixels, and `img.dtype` returns the image datatype.

Arithmetic operations on images

In this section, we will take a look at the various arithmetic operations that can be performed on images. Images are represented as matrices in OpenCV. So, arithmetic operations on images are the same as arithmetic operations on matrices. Images must be of the same size in order to perform arithmetic operations with images, and these operations are performed on individual pixels .`cv2.add()` method is used to add two images, where images are passed as parameters.

The `cv2.subtract()` method is used to subtract one image from another.

> We know that subtraction operation is not commutative; so, `cv2.subtract(img1,img2)` and `cv2.(img2,img1)` will yield different results, whereas `cv2.add(img1,img2)` and `cv2.add(img2,img1)` will yield the same result as the addition operation is commutative. Both the images have to be of the same size and type as that explained earlier.

Check out the following code:

```
import cv2
img1 = cv2.imread('4.2.03.tiff',1)
img2 = cv2.imread('4.2.04.tiff',1)
cv2.imshow('Image1',img1)
cv2.waitKey(0)
cv2.imshow('Image2',img2)
cv2.waitKey(0)
cv2.imshow('Addition',cv2.add(img1,img2))
cv2.waitKey(0)
cv2.imshow('Image1-Image2',cv2.subtract(img1,img2))
cv2.waitKey(0)
cv2.imshow('Image2-Image1',cv2.subtract(img2,img1))
cv2.waitKey(0)
cv2.destroyAllWindows()
```

The preceding code demonstrates the usage of arithmetic functions on images. Image2 is the same *Lena* image that we experimented with in the previous chapter, so I am not including its output window. The following is the output window of **Image1**:

The following is the output of the **Addition**:

The following is the output window of **Image1-Image2**:

The following is the output window if **Image2-Image1**:

Splitting and merging image color channels

On several occasions, we might be interested in working separately with the red, green, and blue channels. For example, we might want to build a histogram for each channel of an image.

The `cv2.split()` method is used to split an image into three different intensity arrays for each color channel, whereas `cv2.merge()` is used to merge different arrays into a single multichannel array, that is, a color image. Let's take a look at an example:

```
import cv2
img = cv2.imread('4.2.03.tiff',1)
b,g,r = cv2.split (img)
cv2.imshow('Blue Channel',b)
cv2.imshow('Green Channel',g)
cv2.imshow('Red Channel',r)
img=cv2.merge((b,g,r))
cv2.imshow('Merged Output',img)
cv2.waitKey(0)
cv2.destroyAllWindows()
```

The preceding program first splits the image into three channels (blue, green, and red) and then displays each one of them. The separate channels will only hold the intensity values of that color, and they will be essentially displayed as grayscale intensity images. Then, the program will merge all the channels back into an image and display it.

Negating an image

In mathematical terms, the negative of an image is the inversion of colors. For a grayscale image, it is even simpler! The negative of a grayscale image is just the intensity inversion, which can be achieved by finding the complement of the intensity from 255. A pixel value ranges from 0 to 255 and, therefore, negation is the subtraction of the pixel value from the maximum value, that is, 255. The code for this is as follows:

```
import cv2
img = cv2.imread('4.2.07.tiff')
grayscale = cv2.cvtColor(img,cv2.COLOR_BGR2GRAY)
negative = abs(255-grayscale)
cv2.imshow('Original',img)
cv2.imshow('Grayscale',grayscale)
cv2.imshow('Negative',negative)
cv2.waitKey(0)
cv2.destroyAllWindows()
```

The negative of a negative will be the original grayscale image. Try this on your own by taking the image negative of a negative again.

Logical operations on images

OpenCV provides bitwise logical operation functions on images. We will take a look at functions that provide bitwise logical AND, OR, XOR (exclusive OR), and NOT (inversion) functionalities. These functions can be better demonstrated visually with grayscale images. I am going to use barcode images in horizontal and vertical orientations for demonstration. Look at the following code:

```
import cv2
import matplotlib.pyplot as plt

img1 = cv2.imread('Barcode_Hor.png',0)
img2 = cv2.imread('Barcode_Ver.png',0)
not_out=cv2.bitwise_not(img1)
and_out=cv2.bitwise_and(img1,img2)
or_out=cv2.bitwise_or(img1,img2)
xor_out=cv2.bitwise_xor(img1,img2)

titles = ['Image 1','Image 2','Image 1 NOT','AND','OR','XOR']
images = [img1,img2,not_out,and_out,or_out,xor_out]

for i in xrange(6):
    plt.subplot(2,3,i+1)
    plt.imshow(images[i],cmap='gray')
    plt.title(titles[i])
    plt.xticks([]),plt.yticks([])
plt.show()
```

We first read images in the grayscale mode and calculate the NOT, AND, OR, and XOR, and then, with `matplotlib`, we display them in a neat way. We are leveraging the `plt.subplot()` function here to display multiple images. In this example, we are creating a two row and three column grid for our images and displaying each image in every part of the grid. You can modify this line and make it `plt.subplot(3,2,i+1)` in order to create a three row and two column grid.

We can do this without a loop in the following way. For each image, you have to write the following statements. I am writing this for the first image here only. Go ahead and write it for the rest of the five images:

```
plt.subplot(2,3,1) , plt.imshow(img1,cmap='gray') , plt.title('Image
1') , plt.xticks([]),plt.yticks([])
```

Finally, use `plt.show()` to display. This technique is to avoid the loop where there is very small number of images to be displayed: usually 2 or 3. The output of this will be exactly the same, as follows:

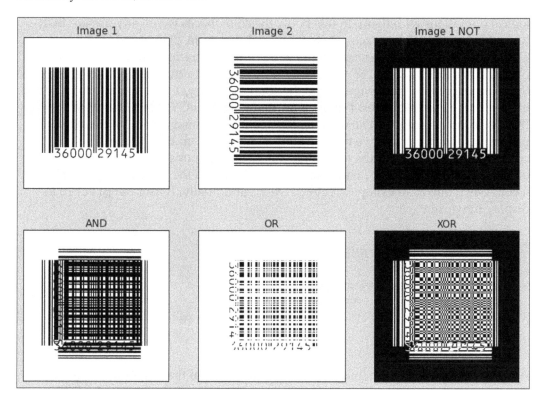

 You might want to make a note of the fact that a logical NOT operation is the negative of the image.

You can check out the Python OpenCV API documentation at `http://docs.opencv.org/modules/refman.html`.

Colorspaces and conversions

A **colorspace** is a mathematical model used to represent colors. Usually, colorspaces are used to represent colors in a numerical form and perform mathematical and logical operations with them. In this book, the colorspaces we mostly use are BGR (OpenCV's default colorspace), RGB, HSV, and grayscale. BGR stand for Blue, Green, and Red. HSV represents colors in the Hue, Saturation, and Value format. OpenCV has a `cv2.cvtColor(img,conv_flag)` function that allows us to change the colorspace of an `img` image, while the source and target colorspaces are indicated in the `conv_flag` parameter. We have learned that OpenCV loads images in the BGR format, and `matplotlib` uses the RGB format for images. So, before displaying images with `matplotlib`, we need to convert images from BGR to the RGB colorspace. Take a look at the following code. The programs read image in the color mode using `cv2.imread()`, which imports the image in the BGR colorspace. Then, it converts it into RGB using `cv2.cvtColor()`, and finally, it uses `matplotlib` to display the image:

```
import cv2
import matplotlib.pyplot as plt

img = cv2.imread('4.2.07.tiff',1)
img = cv2.cvtColor( img , cv2.COLOR_BGR2RGB )
plt.imshow( img ), plt.title('COLOR IMAGE'), plt.xticks([]),
   plt.yticks([])
plt.show()
```

Another way to convert an image from BGR to RGB is to first split the image into three separate channels (B, G, and R channels) and merge them in the BGR order. However, this takes more time as split and merge operations are inherently computationally costly, making them slower and inefficient. The following code shows this method:

```
import cv2
import matplotlib.pyplot as plt
img = cv2.imread('4.2.07.tiff',1)
b,g,r = cv2.split( img )
img=cv2.merge((r,g,b))
plt.imshow( img ), plt.title('COLOR IMAGE'), plt.xticks([]),
   plt.yticks([])
plt.show()
```

The output of both the programs is the same as that shown in the following screenshot:

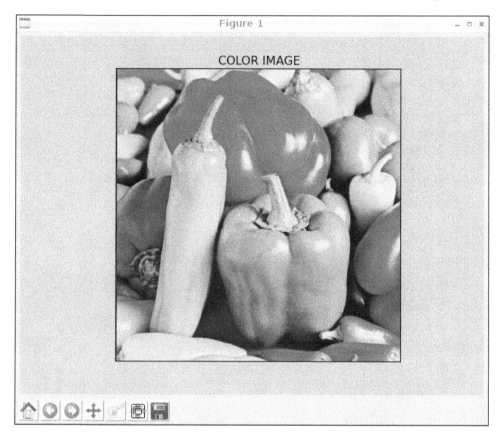

If you need to know the colorspace conversion flags, then the following snippet of code will assist you in finding the list of available flags for your current OpenCV installation:

```
import cv2
j=0
for filename in dir(cv2):
    if filename.startswith('COLOR_'):
        print filename
        j=j+1

print 'There are ' + str(j) + ' Colorspace Conversion flags in
    OpenCV'
```

The last few lines of the output will be as follows (I am not including the complete output due to space limitation):

```
                  .

                  .

                  .

COLOR_YUV420P2BGRA
COLOR_YUV420P2GRAY
COLOR_YUV420P2RGB
COLOR_YUV420P2RGBA
COLOR_YUV420SP2BGR
COLOR_YUV420SP2BGRA
COLOR_YUV420SP2GRAY
COLOR_YUV420SP2RGB
COLOR_YUV420SP2RGBA
There are 176 Colorspace Conversion flags in OpenCV
```

The following code converts a color from BGR to HSV and prints it:

```
>>> import cv2
>>> import numpy as np
>>> c =  cv2.cvtColor(np.uint8[[[255,0,0]]]),cv2.COLOR_BGR2HSV)
>>> print c
[[[120 255 255]]]
```

The preceding snippet of code prints an HSV value of Blue represented in BGR.

Hue, Saturation, Value (HSV) is a color model that describes colors (hue or tint) in terms of their shade (the saturation or the amount of gray) and their brightness (the value or luminance). Hue is expressed as a number representing hues of red, yellow, green, cyan , blue, and magenta. Saturation is the amount of gray in the color. Value works in conjunction with saturation and describes the brightness or intensity of the color.

Tracking in real time based on color

Let's study a real-life application of this concept. In the HSV format, it's much easier to recognize the color range. If we need to track a specific color object, we will need to define a color range in HSV and then convert the captured image in the HSV format and check whether the part of that image falls within the HSV color range of our interest. We can use the cv2.inRange() function to achieve this. This function takes an image, the upper and lower bounds of the colors, and then it checks the range criteria for each pixel. If the pixel value falls in the given color range, then the corresponding pixel in the output image is 0; otherwise, it is 255, thus creating a binary mask. We can use bitwise_and() to extract the color range we're interested in using this binary mask thereafter. Take a look at the following code to understand this concept:

```
import numpy as np
import cv2

cam = cv2.VideoCapture(0)

while (True):
    ret, frame = cam.read()

hsv = cv2.cvtColor(frame, cv2.COLOR_BGR2HSV)

image_mask = cv2.inRange(hsv, np.array([40, 50, 50]),
    np.array([80, 255, 255]))

output = cv2.bitwise_and(frame, frame, mask = image_mask)

cv2.imshow('Original', frame)
cv2.imshow('Output', output)

if cv2.waitKey(1) == 27:
    break

cv2.destroyAllWindows()
cam.release()
```

We're tracking the green-colored objects in this program. The output should be similar to the following figure. I used green tea bag tags as the test object.

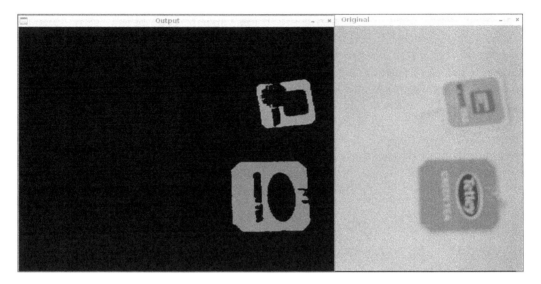

The mask image is not included in the preceding figure. You can see it yourself by adding cv2.imshow('Image Mask',image_mask) to the code. It will be a binary (pure black and white) image.

We can also track multiple colors by tweaking this code a bit. We need to modify the preceding code by creating a mask for another color range. Then, we can use cv2.add() to get the combined mask for two distinct color ranges, as follows:

```
blue=cv2.inRange(hsv, np.array([100,50,50]),
  np.array([140,255,255]))
green=cv2.inRange(hsv,np.array([40,50,50]),np.array([80,255,255]))
image_mask=cv2.add(blue,green)
output=cv2.bitwise_and(frame,frame,mask=image_mask)
```

Try this code and check the output by yourself.

Summary

In this chapter, we learned the basics of computer vision with OpenCV and Pi. We also went through the basic image processing operations and implemented a real-life project to track objects in a live video stream based on the color.

In the next chapter, we will learn some more advanced concepts in computer vision and implement a fully fledged motion detection system with Pi and a webcam with the use of these concepts.

8
Creating Your Own Motion Detection and Tracking System

In the previous chapter, we studied the basics of the OpenCV library. We set up our Pi for OpenCV programming with Python and implemented a simple project to track an object based on the color in OpenCV with a live webcam feed. In this chapter, we will learn about some more advanced concepts and implement one more project based on OpenCV. In this chapter, we will learn about the following topics:

- Thresholding
- Noise reduction
- Morphological operations on images
- Contours in OpenCV
- Real-time motion detection and tracking

Thresholding images

Thresholding is a way to segment images. Although thresholding methods and algorithms are available for colored images, it works best on grayscale images. Thresholding usually (but not always) converts grayscale images into binary images (in a binary image, each pixel can have only one of the two possible values: white or black). Thresholding the image is usually the first step in many image processing applications.

The way thresholding works is very simple. We define a threshold value. For a pixel in a grayscale image, if the value of grayscale intensity is greater than the threshold, then we assign a value to the pixel (for example, white); otherwise, we assign a black value to the pixel. This is the simplest form of thresholding. Also, there are many other variations of this method, which we will look at now.

In OpenCV, the `cv2.threshold()` function is used to threshold images. Its input includes grayscale image, threshold values, `maxVal`, and threshold methods as parameters and returns the thresholded image as the output. `maxVal` is the value assigned to the pixel if the pixel intensity is greater (or lesser in some methods) than the threshold. There are many threshold methods available in OpenCV; in the beginning, the simplest form of thresholding we saw was `cv2.THRESH_BINARY`. Let's look at the mathematical representation of some of the threshold methods.

Say (x,y) is the input pixel; then, operations for threshold methods will be as follows:

- `cv2.THRESH_BINARY`

  If `intensity(x,y) >` `threshold,` then set `intensity(x,y) =maxVal;` else, set `intensity(x,y) = 0`

- `cv2.THRESH_BINARY_INV`

  If `intensity(x,y) >` `threshold,` then set `intensity(x,y) =0;` else, set `intensity(x,y) = maxVal`

- `cv2.THRESH_TRUNC`

  If `intensity(x,y) >` `threshold,` then set `intensity(x,y) =threshold;` else, leave `intensity(x,y)` as it is

- `cv2.THRESH_TOZERO`

  If `intensity(x,y) >` `threshold,` then leave `intensity(x,y)` as it is; else, set `intensity(x,y) = 0`

- `cv2.THRESH_TOZERO_INV`

  If `intensity(x,y) >` `threshold,` then set `intensity(x,y) =0;` else, leave `intensity(x,y)` as it is

The demonstration of the threshold functionality usually works best on grayscale images with a gradually increasing gradient. In the following example, we are setting the value of the threshold as `127`, so the image is segmened in two sets of pixels depending on the value of their intensity:

```
import cv2
import matplotlib.pyplot as plt
```

```
img = cv2.imread('gray21.512.tiff',0)
th=127
max_val=255
ret,o1 = cv2.threshold(img,th,max_val,cv2.THRESH_BINARY)
ret,o2 = cv2.threshold(img,th,max_val,cv2.THRESH_BINARY_INV)
ret,o3 = cv2.threshold(img,th,max_val,cv2.THRESH_TOZERO)
ret,o4 = cv2.threshold(img,th,max_val,cv2.THRESH_TOZERO_INV)
ret,o5 = cv2.threshold(img,th,max_val,cv2.THRESH_TRUNC)

titles = ['Input Image','BINARY','BINARY_INV','TOZERO',
          'TOZERO_INV','TRUNC']
output = [img, o1, o2, o3, o4, o5]

for i in xrange(6):
    plt.subplot(2,3,i+1),plt.imshow(output[i],cmap='gray')
plt.title(titles[i])
plt.xticks([]),plt.yticks([])
plt.show()
```

The output of the preceding code will be as follows:

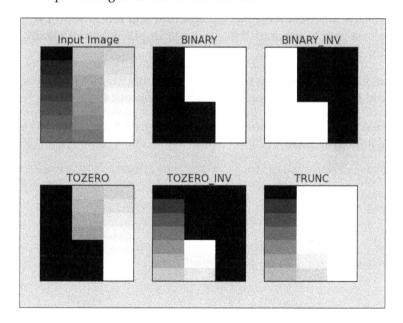

Otsu's method

Otsu's method for thresholding automatically determines the value of the threshold for images that have two peaks in their histogram (bimodal histograms). The following is a bimodal histogram:

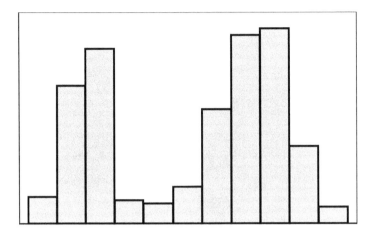

This usually means that the image has background and foreground pixels and Otsu's method is the best way to separate these two sets of pixels automatically without specifying a threshold value.

Otsu's method is not the best way for those images that are not in the background and foreground model and may provide improper output if applied.

This method is applied in addition to other methods, and the threshold is passed as 0. Try out the following code:

```
ret,output=cv2.threshold(image,0,255,cv2.THRESH_BINARY+cv2.THRESH_
OTSU)
```

The output of this will be as follows. This is a screenshot of a tank in a desert:

Noise

Noise means an unwanted signal. Image/video noise means unwanted variations in intensity (for grayscale image) or colors (for color images) that are not present in the real object being photographed or recorded. Image noise is a form of electronic disruption and could come from many sources, such as camera sensors and circuitry in digital or analog cameras. Noise in digital cameras is equivalent to the film grain of analog cameras. Though some noise is always present in any output of electronic devices, a high amount of image noise considerably degrades the overall image quality, making it useless for the intended purpose. To represent the quality of the electronic output (in our case, digital images), the mathematical term **signal-to-noise ratio (SNR)** is a very useful term. Mathematically, it's defined as follows:

$$SNR = \frac{SignalPower}{NoisePower}$$

 More signal-to-noise ratio translates into better quality image.

Kernels for noise removal

In the following concepts and their implementations, we are going to use kernels. **Kernels** are square matrices used in image processing. We can apply a kernel to an image to get different results, such as the blurring, smoothing, edge detection, and sharpening of an image. One of the main uses of kernels is to apply a low pass filter to an image. Low pass filters average out rapid changes in the intensity of the image pixels. This basically smoothens or blurs the image. A simple averaging kernel can be mathematically represented as follows:

$$K = \frac{All\ Ones\ Matrix}{Rows * Cols}$$

For row = cols = 3, kernel will be as follows:

$$K = \frac{\begin{bmatrix} 1 & 1 & 1 \\ 1 & 1 & 1 \\ 1 & 1 & 1 \end{bmatrix}}{9}$$

The value of the rows and columns in the kernel is always odd.

We can use the following NumPy code to create this kernel:

```
K=np.ones((3,3),np.uint32)/9
```

2D convolution filtering

`cv2.filter2D()` function convolves the previously mentioned kernel with the image, thus applying a linear filter to the image. This function accepts the source image and depth of the destination image (-1 in our case, where -1 means the same depth as the source image) and a kernel. Take a look at the following code. It applies a 7 x 7 averaging filter to an image:

```
import cv2
importnumpy as np
frommatplotlib import pyplot as plt

img = cv2.imread('4.2.03.tiff',1)

input = cv2.cvtColor(img,cv2.COLOR_BGR2RGB)
output = cv2.filter2D(input,-1,np.ones((7,7),np.float32)/49)

plt.subplot(121),plt.imshow(input),plt.title('Input')
plt.xticks([]), plt.yticks([])
plt.subplot(122),plt.imshow(output),plt.title('Output')
plt.xticks([]), plt.yticks([])
plt.show()
```

The output will be a filtered image, as follows:

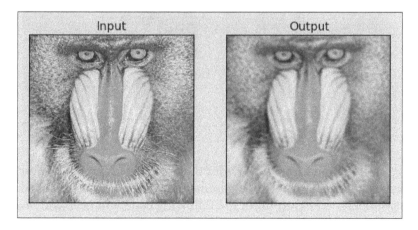

Low pass filtering

As discussed in the kernels section, low pass filters are excellent when it comes to removing sharp components (high frequency information) such as edges and noise and retaining low frequency information (so-called low pass filters), thus blurring or smoothening them.

Let's explore the low pass filtering functions available in OpenCV. We do not have to create and pass the kernel as an argument to these functions; instead, these functions create the kernel based on the size of the kernel we pass as the parameter.

`cv2.boxFilter()` function takes the image, depth, and size of the kernel as inputs and blurs the image. We can specify `normalize` as either `True` or `False`. If it's `True`, the matrix in the kernel would have $\frac{1}{rows*cols}$ as its coefficient; thus, the matrix is called a normalized box filter. If `normalize` is `False`, then the coefficient will be 1, and it will be an unnormalized box filter. An unnormalized box filter is useful for the computing of various integral characteristics over each pixel neighborhood, such as covariance matrices of image derivatives (used in dense optical flow algorithms, and so on). The following code demonstrates a normalized box filter:

```
output=cv2.boxFilter(input,-1,(3,3),normalize=True)
```

The output of the code will be as follows, and it will have less smoothing than the previous one due to the size of the kernel matrix:

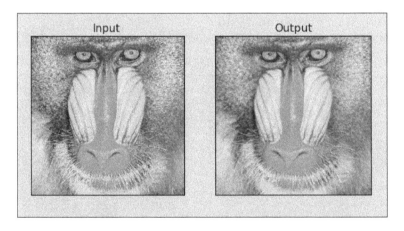

The `cv2.blur()` function directly provides the normalized box filter by accepting the input image and the kernel size as parameters without the need to specify the `normalize` parameter. The output for the following code will be exactly the same as the preceding output:

```
output = cv2.blur(input,(3,3))
```

As an exercise, try passing `normalize` as `False` for an unnormalised box filter to `cv2.boxFilter()` and view the output.

The `cv2.GaussianBlur()` function uses the Gaussian kernel in place of the box filter to be applied. This filter is highly effective against Gaussian noise. The following is the code that can be used for this function:

```
output = cv2.GaussianBlur(input,(3,3),0)
```

 You might want to read more about Gaussian noise at `http://homepages.inf.ed.ac.uk/rbf/HIPR2/noise.htm`.

The following is the output of the earlier code where the input is the image with Gaussian noise and the output is the image with removed Gaussian noise.

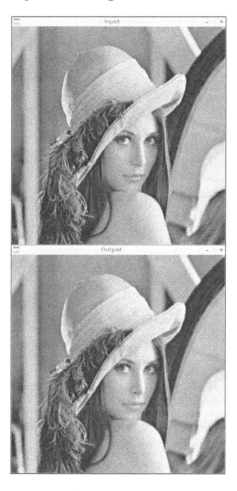

`cv2.medianBlur()` is used for the median blurring of the image using the median filter. It calculates the median of all the values under the kernel, and the center pixel in the kernel is replaced with the calculated median. In this filter, a window slides along the image, and the median intensity value of the pixels within the window becomes the output intensity of the pixel being processed. This is highly effective against salt and pepper noise. We need to pass an input image and an odd positive integer (not the rows, columns tuple like the previous two functions) to this function. The following code introduces salt and pepper noise in the image and then applies `cv2.medianBlur()` to that in order to remove the noise:

```
import cv2
importnumpy as np
import random
frommatplotlib
import pyplot as plt

img = cv2.imread('lena_color_512.tif', 1)

input = cv2.cvtColor(img, cv2.COLOR_BGR2RGB)

output = np.zeros(input.shape, np.uint8)
p = 0.2# probablity of noise
fori in range(input.shape[0]):
    for j in range(input.shape[1]):
    r = random.random()
if r < p / 2:
    output[i][j] = 0, 0, 0
elif r < p:
    output[i][j] = 255, 255, 255
else :
    output[i][j] = input[i][j]

noise_removed = cv2.medianBlur(output, 3)

plt.subplot(121), plt.imshow(output), plt.title('Noisy Image')
plt.xticks([]), plt.yticks([])
plt.subplot(122), plt.imshow(noise_removed), plt.title('Median
    Filtering')
plt.xticks([]), plt.yticks([])
plt.show()
```

You will find that the salt and pepper noise is drastically reduced and the image is much more comprehensible to the human eye.

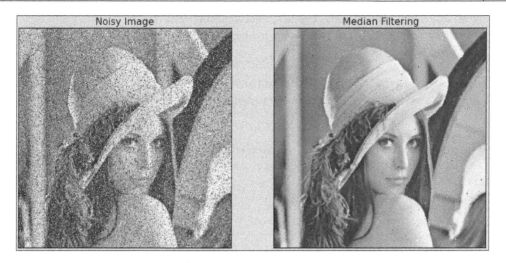

Morphological transformations on images

Morphological operations are based on image shapes, and they work best on binary images. We can use these to get away with a lot of unwanted information, such as noise in an image. Any morphological operation requires two inputs: image and kernel. In this section, we will explore the erosion, dilation, and gradient of an image. Since binary images are most suitable for explaining this concept, we will use a binary image (black and white) to study the concepts.

Erosion removes the boundaries in the image and slims it. In a binary image, white is the foreground and black is the background. All the pixels at the boundary of the white foreground image are made zero, thus slimming the image and eroding away the boundary. Dilation is exactly opposite of erosion; it expands the foreground image boundary and flattens it. The extent of to erosion and dilation depends on the kernel and the number of iterations. The morphological gradient of an image is the difference between dilation and erosion. It will return the outline of an image. Check out the following code for the basic usage of these operations in OpenCV. We will be using these in our next chapter to refine our image for better output:

```
import numpy as np
import cv2
from matplotlib import pyplot as plt

img = cv2.imread('morphological.tif',0)
kernel = np.ones((5,5),np.uint8)
```

```
erosion = cv2.erode(img,kernel,iterations = 2)
dilation = cv2.dilate(img,kernel,iterations = 2)
gradient = cv2.morphologyEx(img, cv2.MORPH_GRADIENT, kernel)

titles=['Original','Erosion','Dilation','Gradient']
output=[img,erosion,dilation,gradient]

for i in xrange(4):
    plt.subplot(2,2,i+1),plt.imshow(output[i],cmap='gray')
    plt.title(titles[i]),plt.xticks([]),plt.yticks([])
plt.show()
```

The output will be as follows:

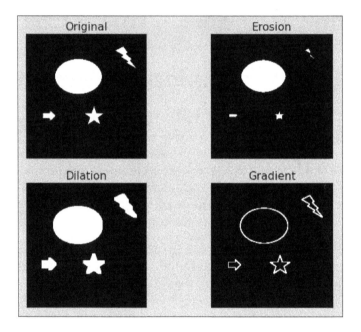

Motion detection and tracking

We will now build a sophisticated motion detection and tracking system with simple logic to find the difference between subsequent frames from a video feed, such as a webcam stream and plotting contours around the area where the difference is detected.

Let's import the required libraries and initialize the webcam:

```
import cv2
import numpy as np

cap = cv2.VideoCapture(0)
```

We will need a kernel for the dilation operation that we will create in advance rather than creating it every time in the loop:

```
k=np.ones((3,3),np.uint8)
```

The following code will capture and store the subsequent frames:

```
t0 = cap.read()[1]
t1 = cap.read()[1]
```

Now we initiate the `while` loop and calculate the difference between the frames and convert the output to grayscale for further processing:

```
while(True):

    d=cv2.absdiff(t1,t0)

    grey = cv2.cvtColor(d, cv2.COLOR_BGR2GRAY)
```

The output will be as follows, and it shows difference of pixels between the frames:

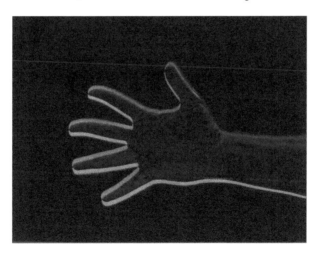

This image might contain some noise, so we will blur it first:

```
blur = cv2.GaussianBlur(grey,(3,3),0)
```

We use binary threshold to convert this noise-removed output into a binary image with the following code:

```
ret, th = cv2.threshold( blur, 15, 255, cv2.THRESH_BINARY )
```

The final operation will be to dilate the image so that it will be easier for us to find the boundary clearly:

```
dilated=cv2.dilate(th,k,iterations=2)
```

The output of the preceding step will be the following:

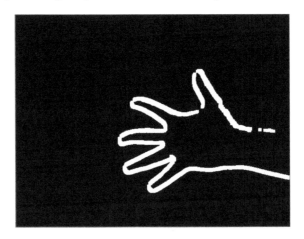

Then, we find and draw the contours for the preceding image with the following code:

```
contours, hierarchy =
cv2.findContours(dilated,cv2.RETR_TREE,cv2.CHAIN_APPROX_SIMPLE)

t2=t0
cv2.drawContours(t2, contours, -1, (0,255,0), 2 )

cv2.imshow('Output', t2 )
```

Finally, we assign the latest frame to the older frame and capture the next frame with the webcam with the following code:

```
t0=t1
t1=cap.read()[1]
```

We terminate the loop once we detect the *Esc* keypress, as usual:

```
if cv2.waitKey(5) == 27 :
    break
```

Once the loop is terminated, we release the camera and destroy the display window:

```
cap.release()
cv2.destroyAllWindows()
```

This will draw the contour roughly around the area where the movement is detected, as shown in the following screenshot:

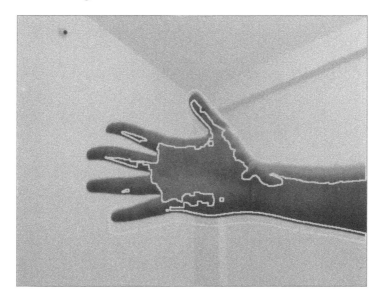

This code works very well for slow movements. You can make the output more interesting by drawing contours with different colors. Also, you can find out the centroid of the contours and draw crosshairs or circles corresponding to the centroids.

 If you wish to explore OpenCV with Raspberry Pi in more depth, go through *Raspberry Pi Computer Vision Programming*. Here is the link: https://www.packtpub.com/hardware-and-creative/raspberry-pi-computer-vision-programming.

Summary

In this chapter, we learned about the advanced topics of computer vision with OpenCV and Pi.

We learned about advanced image processing techniques, such as thresholding, noise reduction, contours, and morphological operations. Finally, we implemented all these techniques to build a real-life application for image processing.

In the next chapter, we will learn about the basics of interfacing Pi with Grove Shield and Grove Sensors.

9
Grove Sensors and the Raspberry Pi

In the previous chapter, we discussed object detection and tracking and also learned to detect motion in scenes. Along the way, we also learned various concepts of image processing that may also be used for different applications.

In this chapter, we will be moving forward from the software-based approach of the previous chapter and explore the hardware capabilities of the Raspberry Pi. We will also learn about an add-on called the GrovePi Shield, which will extend the GPIO capabilities of the Pi platform and make it even easier to connect new sensors to it. In this chapter, we will learn about the following:

- Introducing the GrovePi Shield and sensors
- Setting up the Shield with the Raspberry Pi
- Building a weather station
- Building an intruder detection system

Introducing the GrovePi

The GrovePi Shield is an open source platform to connect a range of sensors called the Grove sensors to the Raspberry Pi. We can create our own Internet of Things applications without any need for soldering using the GrovePi! Grove is an easy-to-use collection of more than a hundred Plug and Play modules that we can use to sense and interact with the physical world. The array of sensors include relays, temperature sensors, OLED displays, ultrasonic ranger, joystick, accelerometer, humidity sensor, GPS, and so on. They are divided on the basis of the following six categories: Environment Monitoring, Motion Sensing, User Interface, Physical Monitoring, Logic Gate, and Power.

You can interact and monitor the world using the sensors and then store the data on your Raspberry Pi bridging the gap to the real world!

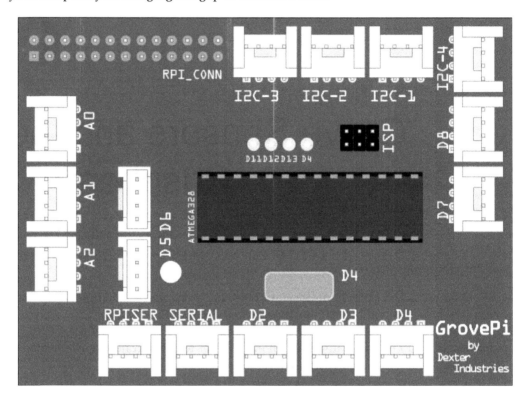

As you can see from the preceding image, the GrovePi slips over the Raspberry Pi and has a variety of sockets to hold the different sensors that you might want to add to your Raspberry Pi. It works with the Raspberry Pi models A, A+, B, B+, 2, and uses an open source library made available by its creators to allow users to program in Python, C, C++, Go, and NodeJS.

For this chapter, we will need the following components:

- Humidity and temperature sensor (http://www.seeedstudio.com/depot/Grove-TempHumi-Sensor-p-745.html?cPath=25_125)
- LED (http://www.seeedstudio.com/depot/Grove-Red-LED-p-1142.html?cPath=81_35)
- Ultrasonic ranger (http://www.seeedstudio.com/depot/Grove-Ultrasonic-Ranger-p-960.html?cPath=25_31)

- OLED display (http://www.seeedstudio.com/depot/Grove-OLED-Display-096-p-824.html?cPath=34_36)

- Buzzer (http://www.seeedstudio.com/depot/Grove-Buzzer-p-768.html?cPath=38)

- GrovePi+ (http://www.seeedstudio.com/depot/GrovePi-p-2241.html)

All of the preceding are available on the SeeedStudio website.

You can find out more about the GrovePi and the sensors on their creator's website:

http://www.dexterindustries.com/

Setting up the GrovePi

Let us have a look at an image of the GrovePi:

As you can see from the preceding image, GrovePi has a socket that allows it to fit directly over the Raspberry Pi. Once we do that, we can begin to set up the software on the Raspberry Pi to use the shield. The steps are given next.

1. Turn on the Raspberry Pi without the GrovePi attached and open a terminal window either by using a monitor or through ssh:

```
The authenticity of host '192.168.1.5 (192.168.1.5)' can't be established.
ECDSA key fingerprint is 09:e5:6a:c3:01:5f:79:84:78:49:43:f4:43:55:1d:31.
Are you sure you want to continue connecting (yes/no)? yes
Warning: Permanently added '192.168.1.5' (ECDSA) to the list of known hosts.
pi@192.168.1.5's password:
Linux raspberrypi 3.18.11+ #781 PREEMPT Tue Apr 21 18:02:18 BST 2015 armv6l

The programs included with the Debian GNU/Linux system are free software;
the exact distribution terms for each program are described in the
individual files in /usr/share/doc/*/copyright.

Debian GNU/Linux comes with ABSOLUTELY NO WARRANTY, to the extent
permitted by applicable law.
Last login: Sat Oct 24 08:17:37 2015
pi@raspberrypi ~ $
```

2. It is recommended that we install GrovePi on the desktop so we first cd into the desktop directory with the following command:

```
$ cd /home/pi/Desktop
```

3. Now clone the repository from GitHub into the desktop with the following command:

```
$ sudo git clone https://github.com/DexterInd/GrovePi
```

```
pi@raspberrypi ~/Desktop $ sudo git clone https://github.com/DexterInd/GrovePi
Cloning into 'GrovePi'...
remote: Counting objects: 2653, done.
remote: Total 2653 (delta 0), reused 0 (delta 0), pack-reused 2653
Receiving objects: 100% (2653/2653), 1.80 MiB | 29 KiB/s, done.
Resolving deltas: 100% (1424/1424), done.
pi@raspberrypi ~/Desktop $
```

4. We are now ready to execute the install script for the GrovePi. But we must first make the script executable and then run it:

```
$ cd /home/pi/Desktop/GrovePi/Script
$ sudo chmod +x install.sh
$ sudo ./install.sh
```

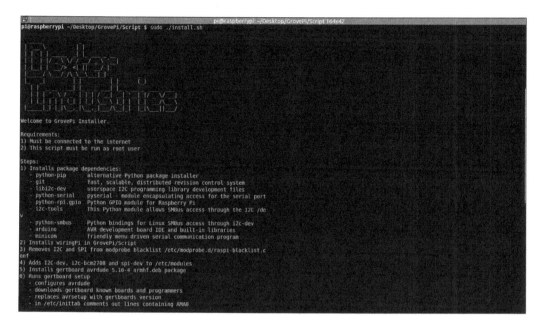

5. The terminal will ask you to press *ENTER* and subsequently *Y* to continue, so please do press *Enter* to install all the required packages.

The setup will now be completed and your Raspberry Pi will be restarted automatically. With the Raspberry Pi powered off, attach the GrovePi and then turn it on.

```
Making libraries global . . .
==============================
Please restart to implement changes!

  | □ | \ |   | / |   | /\ |   | □ |
  | □ |  \|   | \ |   | /\ |   | □ |
  | \ |  /    |  /|   | /  \ |  | \ |

Please restart to implement changes!
To Restart type sudo reboot
To finish changes, we will reboot the Pi.
Pi must reboot for changes and updates to take effect.
If you need to abort the reboot, press Ctrl+C.  Otherwise, reboot!
Rebooting in 5 seconds!
Rebooting in 4 seconds!
Rebooting in 3 seconds!
Rebooting in 2 seconds!
Rebooting in 1 seconds!
Rebooting now!  Your Pi wake up with a freshly updated Raspberry Pi!

Broadcast message from root@raspberrypi (pts/1) (Tue Dec  8 11:58:27 2015):
The system is going down for reboot NOW!
```

Now we will check if the Raspberry Pi detected the GrovePi upon reboot. Run:

```
$ sudo i2cdetect -y 1
```

The command `i2cdetect` detects any peripherals that are connected to the I2C Pins of the Raspberry Pi, which are GPIO02 and GPIO03 in the case of Pi B+ and Pi 2. These are the pins that the GrovePi Shield uses to establish a connection to the Raspberry Pi.

In case you have a Raspberry Pi model that was produced before October 2012, you can run the following:

```
$ sudo i2cdetect -y 0
```

```
^Cpi@raspberrypi ~/Desktop/GrovePi/Software/Python $ sudo i2cdetect -y 1
     0  1  2  3  4  5  6  7  8  9  a  b  c  d  e  f
00:        -- 04 -- -- -- -- -- -- -- -- -- -- -- --
10: -- -- -- -- -- -- -- -- -- -- -- -- -- -- -- --
20: -- -- -- -- -- -- -- -- -- -- -- -- -- -- -- --
30: -- -- -- -- -- -- -- -- -- -- -- -- -- -- -- --
40: -- -- -- -- -- -- -- -- -- -- -- -- -- -- -- --
50: -- -- -- -- -- -- -- -- -- -- -- -- -- -- -- --
60: -- -- -- -- -- -- -- -- -- -- -- -- -- -- -- --
70: -- -- -- -- -- -- -- --
```

If you see a '04' in the output matrix, that means the GrovePi is detected by the Raspberry Pi I2C port. We can now test to see if it works properly. To test, connect an LED module to the D4 port and run the LED Blink Python example that comes bundled with the Github repository we cloned in an earlier step. To do that, run the following command:

```
$ cd /home/pi/Desktop/GrovePi/Software/Python
```

```
$ sudo python grove_led_blink.py
```

If everything was installed correctly in the previous steps, the LED on port D4 should now start blinking.

```
pi@raspberrypi ~/Desktop/GrovePi/Software/Python $ sudo python grove_led_blink.py
This example will blink a Grove LED connected to the GrovePi+ on the port labeled
D4.  If you're having trouble seeing the LED blink, be sure to check the LED conne
ction and the port number.  You may also try reversing the direction of the LED or
 the sensor.

Connect the LED to the port labele D4!
LED ON!
LED OFF!
LED ON!
LED OFF!
LED ON!
LED OFF!
```

Congratulations, we have successfully set up the GrovePi to work with the Raspberry Pi and we will now move on to some complex and interesting examples to explore the functionality of the GrovePi.

Displaying the weather

For our first project, we will be using the humidity and temperature sensor of the gross array and use its measurements to be displayed on an OLED display. You will need the two modules and some connection cables to set up the hardware for this project.

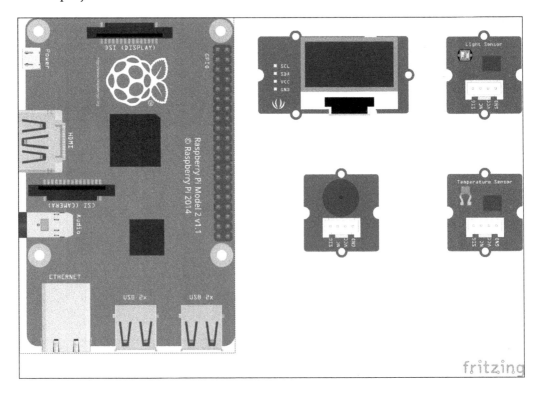

Connect the only display module to any of the three i2c ports on the GrovePi, and connect the humidity and temperature sensor to port D7. Now we will have a look at the following code and then learn what each statement does:

```
from grovepi import *
from grove_oled import *
dht_sensor_port = 7
oled_init()
oled_clearDisplay()
oled_setNormalDisplay()
```

```
oled_setVerticalMode()
time.sleep(.1)
while True:
        try:
            [ temp,hum ] = dht(dht_sensor_port,1)
            print "temp =", temp, "C\thumidity =", hum,"%"
            t = str(temp)
            h = str(hum)
            oled_setTextXY(0,1)
            oled_putString("WEATHER")
            oled_setTextXY(2,0)
            oled_putString("Temp:")
            oled_putString(t+'C')
            oled_setTextXY(3,0)
            oled_putString("Hum :")
            oled_putString(h+"%")
        except (IOError,TypeError) as e:
            print "Error"
```

Save the preceding code as `prog1.py` and run it. You should see the temperature and humidity values being reported on the terminal, as well as on the OLED screen:

```
pi@raspberrypi ~ $ sudo python prog1.py
temp = 24.5 C   humidity = 53.3%
temp = 24.5 C   humidity = 53.3%
temp = 24.5 C   humidity = 53.4%
temp = 24.6 C   humidity = 53.3%
temp = 24.4 C   humidity = 53.3%
temp = 24.5 C   humidity = 53.3%
temp = 24.5 C   humidity = 53.2%
temp = 24.6 C   humidity = 53.3%
```

The first two statements are responsible for importing the dependencies required for the GrovePi Shield and OLED module to work. The asterisk tells Python to import all the classes and functions from the given modules. The second statement creates a variable where the port number for the DHT module is saved. The next statements set up the OLED module for writing data to it. The functions initialize the module, clear the display, and set the vertical mode so that if we write anything subsequently it appears natural. It is recommended that these four statements be executed at the start of any Python program that uses the OLED module.

Next, we add an infinite while loop so that the program keeps on running until the user terminates it. Inside the while loop, we run the code that is responsible for getting the data from the sensor and displaying it on the OLED module. One of the common mistakes when getting data from any source is that the data might not be available. So we always check the validity and availability of data before executing any code to manipulate or use that data. This is why we must add a try catch statement so that if the data is not available, the program does not crash but gives us an error statement.

Inside the try block, our first statement is to get the data from the DHT module using the `dht()` function. This function takes two arguments: the sensor port number and the type of board connected. We'll enter 1 if the board is DHT Pro and 0 if the board is DHT. It also gives us the output in the form of a list containing two elements: the temperature and humidity level.

In the next statement, we print the humidity level and temperature to the terminal so that the user can look at it. The values that we get from the `dht()` command are integers, but to display them on the OLED screen we need to convert them to strings. This is what the `str()` method does. It takes an input like integer, float, list, and so on and gives a string output.

The subsequent commands that begin with `oled_` are all to manipulate the display of the data on the OLED screen. With the `oled_setTextXY()` method, we can set the cursor to display the data. It takes the X and Y coordinates as arguments and sets the cursor there. Next, with the `oled_putString()` method, we actually push the string data to be displayed on the cursor we just set. We do this three times: first to set the title as 'WEATHER', second to set the temperature and its units, and finally to set the humidity and its percentage. Since this method only takes the string as input, it was necessary to convert the integer values of temperature and humidity to the string before using it here.

Finally, we read the last statement that does nothing but handle any error that might be encountered in the `try` block. If it does encounter an error of any sort, it prints **Error** instead of crashing.

We will now move on to our next project, which uses an ultrasonic sensor and a Pi Camera (or a normal webcam if you so choose). Any idea about what we're going to make?

Intruder detection system

Do you have any data that would cause damage if it fell into the wrong hands?
Or do you wish to know who enters a specific place when you're not present?
Well, you can now easily answer these questions by building your own intruder
detection system!

As mentioned before, this project uses an ultrasonic range sensor for the
GrovePi and a PiCam to take pictures if any movement is detected by the ultrasonic
ranger. Connect the ultrasonic ranger to port D4 of the Grove Pi, the buzzer to D5,
the status LED to D3, and the Pi Camera to the port provided on the Raspberry Pi as
learned in *Chapter 4*, *Working with Webcam and Pi Camera*. Following the theme of the
book, we will first look at the whole code, and then learn what each statement does,
line by line:

```python
import picamera
import grovepi
from time import sleep

camera = picamera.PiCamera()
counter = 0
led = 3
buzzer = 5
ultrasonic = 4

while True:
    try:
        if grovepi.ultrasonicRead(ultrasonic) < 100:
        print 'Intruder Detected'
            grovepi.analogWrite(buzzer, 100)
            grovepi.digitalWrite(led, 1)
            sleep(.5)
            grovepi.analogWrite(buzzer, 0)
        grovepi.digitalWrite(led, 0)
            camera.capture('image' + counter + '.jpg')
            print 'Image Captured'
        sleep(2)
    except IOError:
        print "Error"
```

Save the preceding code as `prog2.py` and run it. Now, try to come in front of the ultrasonic sensor and you will see the output on the terminal, and have your picture taken as an intruder!

The code itself is very simple to understand, as it is just an amalgamation of parts from *Chapter 4*, *Working with Webcam and Pi Camera*, which we have already learned, and parts from the previous example. We start by importing the dependencies for the Pi Camera and GrovePi sensors.

As a setting-up step, we set the camera variable to be an object for our Pi Camera and it can be used to take pictures. We set a counter for the number of pictures and set the LED and buzzer to be used on ports D3 and D5 respectively. We also import the sleep method from the 'time' module to add delays. Like before, we include a 'try, except' block in the infinite while loop, so that when errors are encountered, it does not crash.

Basic algorithm for the intruder detection can be described as: Whenever anything comes in front of the ultrasonic ranger whose range is less than 100 cms, it means that there is an intruder. If the preceding condition is true, then sound the buzzer, light the LED, and take a picture. The `ultrasonicRead()` method from the GrovePi module reads the output from the ultrasonic ranger that is connected to port D7 of the GrovePi. If the distance is less than 100 cms, then we proceed to execute the intruder detection alarm procedure. First, we output `Intruder detected` to the terminal, then we turn on the buzzer by the `analogWrite()` method and the LED with the `digitalWrite()` method. The analogue write method takes the port number of the peripheral and a value from 0 to 255. The higher the value, the higher the intensity of the signal transmitted to the peripheral. The `digitalWrite()` method also takes the port number as an input and a binary number, to set the port high or low. We wait for half a second and then turn both the buzzer and LED off. Finally, we capture a photo with the camera pointed toward the direction of the ultrasonic ranger. Congratulations! We now have a photo of the intruder. Now, if we do not add some delay after taking a photo, the code will repeat itself and since the intruder is likely to still be there, the Raspberry Pi may take an unnecessarily large amount of photos. This is likely to burden the CPU and take resources away from other threads that might be running. So we add a two-second delay.

We can also experiment by varying the delay values to see what works best. I leave the reader with an interesting exercise of adding more peripherals to expand the functionality of the system, such as adding a keypad or a switch to turn off the system when it is not required.

Summary

In this chapter, we learned how to connect and interface the GrovePi Shield with the Raspberry Pi, and how to connect the various sensors to it, and use their data to display on external peripherals. We also looked at and understood two examples that can be used easily in real life for useful tasks.

In the next chapter, we will learn about the Internet of Things and how to connect sensors to get the data online and use it effectively. For example, we can extend the intruder detection example and make it such that it e-mails us the photo of the intruder it just took. In this way, we can receive real-time updates from our chosen monitored location. The Internet of Things is a very useful concept and due to the inexpensiveness of the components it takes to get a working system, it is becoming very popular across the globe to make 'dumb' devices 'intelligent'.

10
Internet of Things with the Raspberry Pi

In the previous chapter, we learned to interface different kinds of sensors to the Raspberry Pi to get data from the real world and output some text so that the user can infer the state of his surroundings, such as temperature, humidity, and so on. We also built a surveillance system that takes pictures of any intruder. Now, these are all standalone systems and cannot communicate with any other systems.

In this chapter, we will concentrate on the concept of the *Internet of Things*. This means that we can connect standalone systems, just like the ones we built in the previous chapters, to the Internet. We will connect devices to the Internet and learn how to interact with different *web services*. The following topics will be covered in this chapter:

- Installing the Twitter API for Python
- Using Tweepy
- Setting up a SQLite database
- Building a tweeting weather station

Introducing the Internet of Things

The Internet of Things is all about connecting the devices that were previously not connected to the Internet, in order to make them smarter and more controllable. Since the size and cost of electronic devices are dropping exponentially, we can now afford to incorporate them in our daily use, are garden watering systems, home automation/monitoring systems, and so on. The Internet of Things in this way has opened up a whole host of opportunities, the advantages of which are being taken up by hobbyists, startups, and major companies alike. At the heart of the Internet of Things revolution are small micro computers and sensors that allow these devices to connect to the Internet and exchange data between them.

As mentioned before, in this particular chapter we will extend our previous projects by connecting the Raspberry Pi to the Internet, and make additional projects to demonstrate the capability of the Internet of Things.

We will now learn to exchange data from the Twitter API and post our sensor readings to Twitter.

Installing the Twitter API for Python

API (Application Programming Interface) and it allows developers to communicate with various web services. Since Python is, by default, installed on the Raspberry Pi, we will use a Python script to communicate with the Twitter API over the Web. For this, we will use an open source library called **Tweepy**. It works with Python versions as old as 2.6 and is still under active development. So bugs are likely to be fewer and, if any are found, they are likely to be fixed quickly.

> The GitHub repository for Tweepy can be found at the following link, so that new issues can be submitted and the code can be understood much more clearly:
>
> https://github.com/tweepy/tweepy

We will now proceed to install it and learn how to use it to do things such as sending tweets.

This library can be installed using `pip`, with the following command:

```
sudo pip install python-twitter
```

We can also install bleeding-edge versions of the library by cloning it from GitHub. Run the following command:

```
git clone https://github.com/tweepy/tweepy.git
cd tweepy
sudo python setup.py install
```

 You can also find more information about using Tweepy and the full extent of its capabilities on its official documentation website: `http://tweepy.readthedocs.org/en/v3.5.0/`.

Using Tweepy

Tweepy was built to be easy to set up and use, and in that regard it is of one of the most useable libraries for communicating with the Twitter API. It takes no more than four lines of code to set it up for use. However, before we can use it to communicate with our account on Twitter, we need to set up a developer app on Twitter. For this, we log on to `https://apps.twitter.com`, sign in to our Twitter account and hit **Create New App**, after which we will be greeted by a window that allows us to create a new application, as shown in the following window:

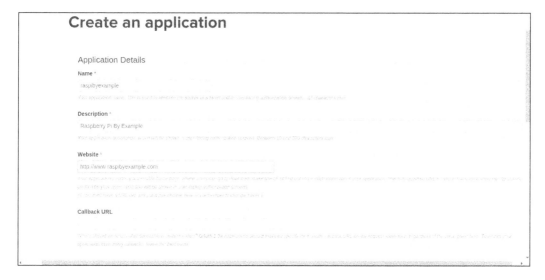

Fill in all the required details such as **Name**, **Description**, and **Website**. Remember, if you don't plan on using this app on a website, you can also put in a placeholder instead of an actual website. Finally, sign the developer agreement and you will have successfully created a Twitter app to use with your Python script. From this app, we will need a Consumer Secret (API Secret) and a Consumer Key (API Key) to use the Tweepy library, which is required for obtaining oauth authentication from the Twitter app. Next, we need to create an access code for our app that is required for communication with the Twitter API.

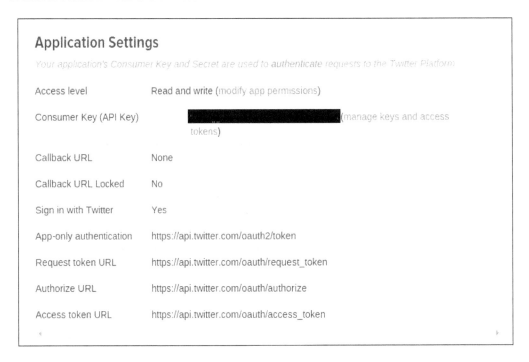

From the preceding page, click the **manage keys and access tokens** to get to the page where you can get your consumer codes and access tokens. The following menu will give the consumer keys:

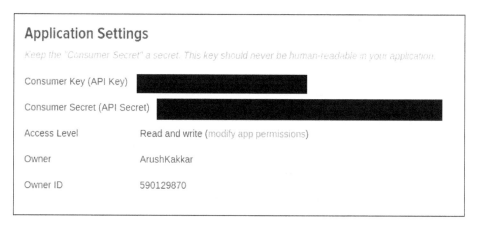

And the following screen will show us our application codes and also give an option to generate new access codes for our application:

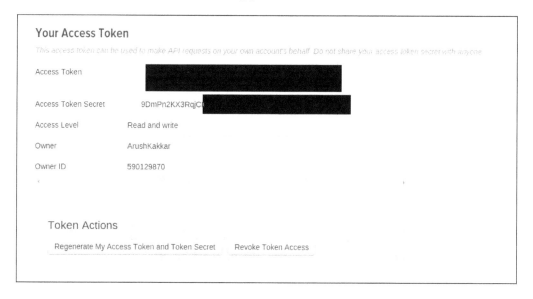

We can now proceed to learn how to use Tweepy to get a list of followers. The code is given next, and the explanation follows:

```
import tweepy

auth = tweepy.OAuthHandler(consumer_key, consumer_secret)
auth.set_access_token(access_token, access_token_secret)

api = tweepy.API(auth)

user = api.get_user('twitter')

print user.screen_name
print user.followers_count
for friend in user.friends():
    print friend.screen_name

api.update_status(' Tweepy says : Hello, world!')
```

In this example, we first import the Tweepy library into Python to use its functionality. We first need to register our Python script (client) to be able to communicate with the Twitter API. For this, we will enter the Consumer Key and the Consumer Secret in the argument of the OAuthHandler method of the Tweepy API. Next, we set the access codes for opening up the Twitter API for our client's use. This is important because we need to have an access token for the app to be able to do things like send tweets, reading tweets, or viewing followers, and so on. Access codes for the Twitter app can be found in its settings, just below the Consumer Codes.

We have so far set the authentication details, but we still need to do the authentication to send tweets. This is accomplished by the API() function in the Tweepy module. We first create an api variable that contains all the methods for interacting with the Twitter API.

The next statement gets the user associated with our unique Consumer Key. Every registered user will have this key and it is unique for every user so they can correctly identify themselves. The get_user() method takes as an argument, the name of the service (Twitter in this case) that we need from the user, and passes the authentication codes that we have got from the previous statement to get the user details. This is stored in the user variable. This variable will have members such as the name, followers, following, and so on.

To check that we really get the correct user from this method, we only need to print the correct members of the user variable. So we first print to the command line, the screen name, and the follower count. The next while loop loops over the `friends()` method of the user variable and stores each follower detail in the friend variable. Then we print the name of each friend to the command line. This way, we can check if we have our user details correct or not.

Finally, we can send a tweet using the `update_status()` method of the Tweepy API. This method takes a string as input and sends out a tweet. However, if a string is more than 140 characters in length, the statement will silently fail that is, it will fail without giving an error.

Now enter your Consumer and Access codes! Save this example as `prog1.py` and run it with the following command:

```
python prog1.py
```

You should see the user details on the terminal, and a tweet from your user:

```
'Tweepy says : Hello, World!'
```

In addition to the preceding functionality, we can also use Tweepy to do other things such as reading statuses. Some of the more important functionality is detailed next:

- `api.home_timeline([since_id], [max_id], [count], [page])`: Returns the 20 most recent tweets on the user's timeline. `count` specifies the number of tweets to retrieve
- `Api.user_timeline([id/user_id/screen_name], [since_id], [max_id], [count], [page])`: Returns the 20 most recent tweets from the specified user or, if none is given, from the authenticating user
- `Api.get_status(id)`: Returns the status by ID
- `Api.update_with_media(filename, [status], [in_reply_to_status_id], [lat], [long], [source], [place_id], [file])`: Updates the authenticated user's status with media

Congratulations! We have successfully set up a Twitter app using Python and communicated with the API. We will now move on to the next example where we learn how to set up a SQLite database to store some data on the Raspberry Pi.

Setting up a SQLite database in Python

SQLite (pronounced **Sequel Lite**) is a lightweight disk-based database that doesn't require a separate server process and uses a modified version of the SQL query language to access the data. The entire database is saved in a single file and can be used for internal data storage. It is also possible to make a prototype of an application using SQLite and then port the code to work with a larger database with minimal modifications. The Python standard library has a module called `sqlite3` included, which is intended to work with this database. This module is SQL interface-compliant with DB-API 2.0.

 You can find more information and the full API reference for the SQLite3 module on its official website: `https://docs.python.org/2/library/sqlite3.html`.

Next is an example on how to use the `sqlite3` module to create a SQLite database to store and retrieve some data. We will go through the code, statement by statement, and analyze what each statement does and also discuss any variations that might be possible.

```
import sqlite3

conn = sqlite3.connect('raspi.db')
cursor = conn.cursor()

#Inserting Data
cursor.execute('''
    CREATE TABLE users(id INTEGER PRIMARY KEY, name TEXT,
                       email TEXT unique, password TEXT)
''')
cursor.execute('''INSERT INTO users(name, email, password)
                      VALUES(?,?,?)''', ('Luke',
                      'luke@skywalker.com', 'iamurfather'))

cursor.execute('''INSERT INTO users(name, email, password)
                      VALUES(?,?,?)''', ('Darth Vader',
                      'darth@vader.com', 'darkside'))

conn.commit()
```

```
#Retrieving Data

user_id = 1
cursor.execute('''SELECT name, email, password FROM users WHERE
id=?''', (user_id,))
user1 = cursor.fetchone()
print(user1[0])
allusers = cursor.fetchall()
for row in allusers:
    print('{0} : {1}, {2}'.format(row[0], row[1], row[2]))




#Deleting or Updating Data

new_email = 'vader@deathstar.com'
userid = 2
cursor.execute('''UPDATE users SET email = ? WHERE id = ? ''',
(new_email, userid))

del_userid = 1
cursor.execute('''DELETE FROM users WHERE id = ? ''',
(del_userid,))

conn.commit()
conn.close()
```

We will now study the data exchanges that took place in the database in the preceding given Python script. Since `sqlite3` is a default Python module, we don't need to install any additional dependencies. So we import the module into our Python program, and create a new file to save the database with the `sqlite.connect()` method. This method creates a new file for the database if none exists, and if it does the method connects to it and loads the existing database inside the file. Next, we create a cursor that acts as a pointer to the data inside the database. As such, we can only manipulate the data that the cursor is pointing to. We do this with the `cursor()` method that operates on the connection variable, which we created in the last statement.

Currently, our file does not have a database, so with the next lines of code we create a database and insert some data in it. The `execute()` method takes SQL commands as one of the arguments to manipulate data. Hence, to create the database, we execute the `CREATE TABLE` query. In this case, we create a table named `users` that will have a minimum of one data column, which is the key number of the data. This ensures that the data has a unique serial ID by which it can be accessed. We save three fields for each user: the name, the e-mail ID, and the password. So this database can be used for logging in to an application where different users can log in. The `TEXT` type in SQL is the same as `str` in Python, `INTEGER` is `int`, `REAL` is `float`. To make sure that no two users enter the same e-mail ID, we add a "unique" marker to the e-mail column. Now that we have created a database, we need to add some data to it. We use the `INSERT INTO` command to accomplish this. After inserting into vi, mention the name of the database into which we want to insert the data with the names of the arguments. Then the values function will take the actual values of the data. The `?` means that the data is given as a value in a tuple. We repeat the same process with different data to add rows to the database. Notice that we didn't need to set the serial ID of the data for it to be saved properly. That is one advantage of having a cursor in the database. It automatically places new data in the next available row in the database. To actually write the data into the database file and save it, we need to commit our changes. This is done by the `commit()` function that operates on the connection variable. You can visualize the database with a free tool called SQLite Database Browser. This is what the database looks like after we have made the changes just specified:

Now that we have learned how to insert new data into the database, we will see how to read existing data from the database.

First, we need to know the serial-id, name, e-mail, or password of the user that we need to retrieve. Let's assume in this case we want to retrieve the user details by the serial ID. So we execute the `SELECT` command, which selects a row based on the condition that is given. If no condition is given, it will automatically select the first row in the database. The whole statement is close to plain English, so should be easy to understand. Basically, it selects the columns specified from the database name that is given according to a condition given after `WHERE`.

So, after the preceding statement our cursor is pointing toward the row whose ID is 1. The `fetchone()` method fetches the data from the row that the cursor is pointing to, and saves it in the `user1` variable as a list. Then, we simply print the first element of the list, which is the user's name in this case. However, if we want to fetch the data from all the rows in the database, we execute the `fetchall()` method. This points the cursor at all the rows in the database starting from the first one, and saves the result in the `allusers` variable. Then, we simply print the data in a `for` loop.

We have now learned how to save and retrieve data from the database. But what if we want to update user details or delete data? The next block of code (in the preceding code snippet) teaches us exactly that.

Assume that we want to update the e-mail ID of the second user in the database. We first set the new e-mail ID in a string variable, and then the user that we want to select in an integer variable. Then, to update the data, we use the UPDATE SQL query. It takes two or more arguments in addition to the database that we want to update: the data that we want to update and a condition, in this case the serial ID of the row. Both of which we give by using the ? technique we described earlier. The condition operator WHERE operates in exactly the same way in UPDATE as it does in SELECT, pointing the cursor according to the condition given. After the update, this is what our table looks like:

To delete some data, we use the DELETE query and select the database with the FROM query. We also employ the condition by using the WHERE query and giving it the serial ID we want to delete.

Since we have changed the data in the database, to write the changes into the file we use the `commit()` method, and finally release the file from the Python script with the `close()` method. This ensures that no new changes can be made to the file unless it is connected again. If we close the file without committing the changes, no changes will be reflected in the database and we will have lost any changes that we previously made. This is what the table looks like after we delete the first row:

Finally, we have learned how to save and update data into a database, and retrieve it on demand for our use. We also know, from our previous Twitter tutorial, how to send updates to Twitter. So for our next project, we will build a tweeting weather station that will also save the data into a database. Sounds interesting? Let's get into it.

Building a tweeting weather station

This is a continuation of the project that we built in the previous chapter and that used the temperature and humidity Grove sensor with the Raspberry Pi to display the weather conditions. We will be using the same hardware.

The only difference now is that instead of displaying the weather on the terminal, we will be live-tweeting it, and also saving the information into a database for later retrieval.

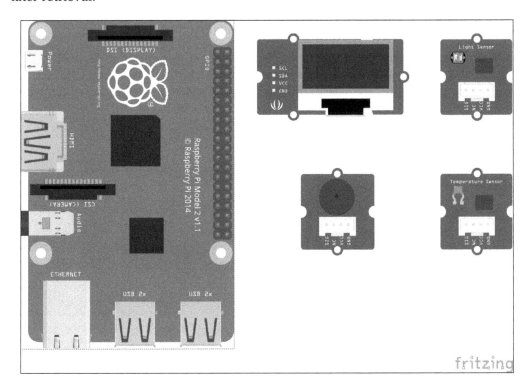

To revisit the project, we should go through it once again by turning to *Chapter 9, Grove Sensors and the Raspberry Pi*. Much of the code that was used previously will be used again, with the addition of the blocks where we tweet the information and save it in a database. For this project, it is recommended that you make a new Twitter account and create a new app on it to get the Consumer and Access codes.

The full Python script is presented next. We know what most of the code does because of the previous projects that we have built, including the weather station, Twitter bot, and SQLite database, but there is a brief summary at the end of the code.

```python
from grovepi import *
from grove_oled import *
import tweepy
import sqlite3
import datetime

dht_sensor_port = 7

oled_init()
oled_clearDisplay()
oled_setNormalDisplay()
oled_setVerticalMode()
time.sleep(.1)

auth = tweepy.OAuthHandler(consumer_key, consumer_secret)
auth.set_access_token(access_token, access_token_secret)
api = tweepy.API(auth)

conn = sqlite3.connect('raspi_weather.db')
cursor = conn.cursor()

cursor.execute('''
    CREATE TABLE weather(id INTEGER PRIMARY KEY, time TEXT,
                         temp INTEGER, hum INTEGER)
''')


while True:
        try:
          [ temp,hum ] = dht(dht_sensor_port,1)
```

```
        print "temp =", temp, "C\thumidity =", hum,"%"
        t = str(temp)
        h = str(hum)
                time = str(datetime.datetime.time(datetime.datetime.
now())))

        oled_setTextXY(0,1)
        oled_putString("WEATHER")

        oled_setTextXY(2,0)
        oled_putString("Temp:")
        oled_putString(t+'C')

        oled_setTextXY(3,0)
        oled_putString("Hum :")
        oled_putString(h+"%")
                api.update_status("Temperature : " + t + " C, " +
                "Humidity : " + h + "% ")
                cursor.execute('''INSERT INTO weather(time, temp,
                hum)
                        VALUES(?,?,?)''', (time, t, h))

        except (IOError,TypeError) as e:
        print "Error"
```

As is evident from the preceding code, it is an updated version of the weather station we built in the previous chapter. We add the consumer and access codes for our Twitter application so that we can tweet the weather information directly from this script. We import the Tweepy library and set up the access. We also import the sqlite3 module and create a new database called weather, which has three data columns: time, temperature, and humidity, in addition to the serial number column. Finally, in addition to displaying the temperature and humidity on the OLED screen, we also update it in our tweet and save it in the database we just created along with the time information. The time information is given by the datetime module that is included with the default Python installation. datetime.datetime.now() gives the current date and time. datetime.datetime.time() gives the current time provided we are only given datetime.datetime.now() as an argument.

The tweets from our script will look like this:

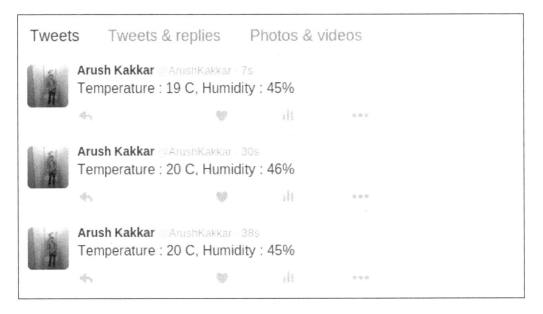

And if we browse the database that we just created, it looks something like this:

	id	time	temp	hum
1	1	13:21:50.708220	20	45
2	2	13:22:13.751878	20	46
3	3	13:22:19.105107	20	45
4	4	13:22:25.720685	20	45
5	5	13:22:30.287131	20	45
6	6	13:22:34.645357	19	47
7	7	13:22:38.839593	20	46
8	8	13:22:42.652832	20	45
9	9	13:22:46.989553	20	45

We have now built a weather station that not only monitors and saves weather information for you but also broadcasts it to the world! An interesting extension to this would be to add speech capabilities so that the Raspberry Pi speaks out the weather information via a speaker. The `espeak` library is an easy-to-use library that accomplishes this easily and effectively. Moreover, you can also hook up to a weather service that has a web API and get your Pi to speak out weather forecasts too!

Adding speech capabilities to our weather station

Speech is one of the many ways in which humans communicate. And it's fascinating to make machines do the things that humans do effortlessly. For precisely that reason, we will add speech capabilities to our tweeting weather station so that it can speak out the weather, and we no longer have to stare at our OLED screen or scroll our Twitter feed to learn about the weather. For this task, we will be using an open source tool called `espeak`, which is a text-to-speech engine and also has an API for Python.

First, install the `espeak` library with the following commands:

```
sudo apt-get install espeak
sudo apt-get install python-espeak
```

The good thing about this library is that we can use it from the terminal or from the Python console. To try it out, make sure that you have a speaker connected to the Pi and execute the following command from the Linux terminal:

```
espeak I will tell you the weather'
```

This will produce the speech output and we will be able to hear it from the speaker. Cool, right?

Next, we will learn how to use it with Python and then also add it to our weather station project. Open a Python console by typing `python` in a Linux terminal. To import the dependencies, execute the following statement:

```
>>> from espeak import espeak
```

This imports the dependencies required for the speech output. Using `espeak` from Python is also as easy as:

```
>>> espeak.synth("I am the weatherman")
```

The `synth` method in the `espeak` module accepts a string and produces speech based on that. It's not the best-sounding voice, but it works!

To add this to the weather station, we can add the following statement inside our while loop:

```
espeak.synth("The current temperature is : " + str(temp))
espeak.synth("Humidity level is : " + str(hum) + "percent")
```

This works because Python supports string concatenation. This means that we can combine two strings just by adding a + sign between them. However, the `temp` and `hum` variables are not string variables. So we need to convert them to strings by the `str()` method. The `Str()` method takes any type of variable and converts it into a string.

We can also use the `espeak` library to tell us many different things about our environment by getting the state from the Grove Sensors.

Summary

In this chapter, we learned how to use Python to communicate with Twitter by using an open source library, Tweepy. We learned how to use Tweepy to send tweets. We also learned how to create a database, save and update data in it, and get some data from an existing database. Toward the end, we extended the capabilities of the weather station we built in *Chapter 9, Grove Sensors and the Raspberry Pi* and added tweeting and data-saving functionalities to it. We also added speech capabilities to it to make it easier to use.

In the next chapter, we will be exploring the interesting topic of parallel computing. We will be using multiple Raspberry Pis to create a cluster of computers that perform computations faster by working in tandem towards a single task. A master Pi will control other slave Pis and outsource its computations to them, so that the task is performed faster. We will use this setup to perform an n-body simulation, which is by itself a very computationally challenging task.

11
Build Your Own Supercomputer with Raspberry Pi

In the previous chapter, we learned how to get the Raspberry Pi to communicate with the Internet, along with some more topics. We learned how to set up the Twitter API and how to send out tweets using it. We also learned how to save data in a database and retrieve it later. Finally, we combined the two concepts and the weather station we built in *Chapter 9, Grove Sensors and the Raspberry Pi* to create a tweeting weather station that also saves the temperature and humidity data in a database.

In all the chapters prior to this one, we explored the Raspberry Pi functionalities. But this chapter will be different in the sense that we will learn how to combine two or more Raspberry Pi devices to create a more powerful computer. Indeed, if you combine enough Raspberry Pi devices, you can make your own supercomputer! Sounds interesting? We will cover the following in this chapter:

- Using a network switch to create a static network for Pi devices
- Installing and setting up MPICH2 and MPI4PY and running on a single node
- Using the static network of multiple Pi devices is to create an **MPI** (short for **Message Parsing Interface**) cluster
- Performance the benchmarking of cluster
- Running GalaxSee (N Body simulation)

Introducing a Pi-based supercomputer

The basic requirements for the building of a supercomputer are as follows:

- Multiple processors
- A mechanism to interconnect them

We already have multiple processors in the form of multiple Raspberry Pi devices. We connect them via a networking hub, which is connected to each Pi via an Ethernet cable. A networking hub is nothing but a router that can accept Ethernet cables. There are dedicated networking hubs that can support many connections but for the purposes of this chapter, we can use a normal Wi-Fi router that accepts four LAN connections in addition to wireless connections. This is because we will not build a cluster of more than four Pi devices. You are welcome to add more devices to this cluster in order to increase your computing power. So, the hardware requirements for this chapter are as follows:

- Three Raspberry Pi devices
- Three Raspbian-installed SD cards
- A networking hub
- Three Ethernet cables
- Power supply for every device

Installing and configuring MPICH2 and MPI4PY

Before we can begin installing the libraries to a network of multiple Pi devices, we need to configure our Raspbian installation to make things a bit easier.

Boot up a Raspberry Pi and in the terminal, enter the following command:

```
sudo raspi-config
```

It is assumed that you have followed all the setup steps that are preferred on first starting up the Raspberry Pi. These are as follows:

1. Expand the filesystem.

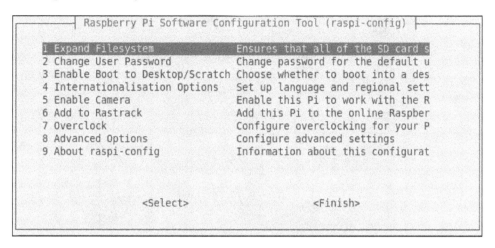

2. Overclock the system (this is optional). We will be using a Pi overclocked to 800MHz as shown below:

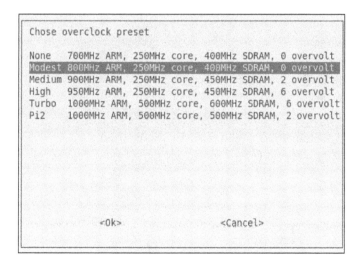

3. Now, enter the advanced menu by selecting **Advanced Options**. We need to configure the following:

    1. Set the hostname to `Pi1`.

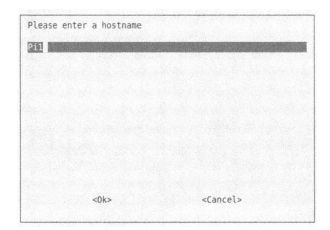

    2. Enable SSH.

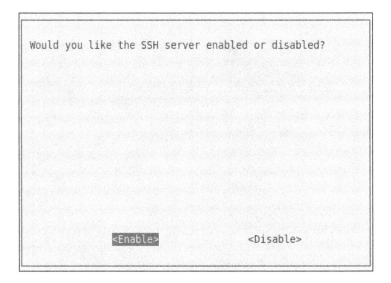

We need to enable auto login so that we do not need to manually log in every Pi once we fire it up. Auto login is enabled by default in the latest versions of the Raspbian operating system, so we don't need to perform the following procedure on the latest version. To enable auto login, exit the configuration menu, but don't reboot yet.
To set the auto login, open the `inittab` file with the following command:

```
sudo nano /etc/inittab
```

Comment out the following line:

```
1:2345:respawn:/sbin/getty --noclear 38400 tty1
```

This is done so that it looks like this:

```
#1:2345:respawn:/sbin/getty --noclear 38400 tty1
```

Then, add the following line:

```
1:2345:respawn:/bin/login -f pi tty1 </dev/tty1 >/dev/tty1 2>&1
```

```
  GNU nano 2.2.6              File: /etc/inittab                    Modified

# Note that on most Debian systems tty7 is used by the X Window System,
# so if you want to add more getty's go ahead but skip tty7 if you run X.
#
#1:2345:respawn:/sbin/getty --noclear 38400 tty1
1:2345:respawn:/bin/login -f pi tty1 </dev/tty1 >/dev/tty1 2>&1
2:23:respawn:/sbin/getty 38400 tty2
3:23:respawn:/sbin/getty 38400 tty3
4:23:respawn:/sbin/getty 38400 tty4
5:23:respawn:/sbin/getty 38400 tty5
6:23:respawn:/sbin/getty 38400 tty6

# Example how to put a getty on a serial line (for a terminal)
#
#T0:23:respawn:/sbin/getty -L ttyS0 9600 vt100
#T1:23:respawn:/sbin/getty -L ttyS1 9600 vt100

# Example how to put a getty on a modem line.
#
#T3:23:respawn:/sbin/mgetty -x0 -s 57600 ttyS3

^G Get Help   ^O WriteOut   ^R Read File  ^Y Prev Page  ^K Cut Text   ^C Cur Pos
^X Exit       ^J Justify    ^W Where Is   ^V Next Page  ^U UnCut Text ^T To Spell
```

Save the file and reboot the Pi with `sudo reboot`. When it boots up, you should be auto-logged in.

We are now ready to proceed and begin installing the software that is required to run a cluster of computers.

Installing the MPICH library

MPICH is a freely available, easily portable, and widely used implementation of the MPI standard, which is a message parsing protocol for distributed memory applications used in parallel computing. Work on the first version of MPICH was started around 1992 and is currently in its third version. MPICH is one of the most popular implementations of the MPI standard due to the fact that it is used as a foundation for a vast majority of MPI implementations, including ones by IBM, Cray, Microsoft, and so on.

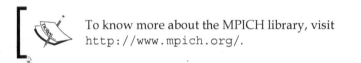

To know more about the MPICH library, visit
`http://www.mpich.org/`.

At the time of writing, the latest version of MPICH is 3.2. The installation instructions for this are presented. However, these should work on all the sub-versions of MPICH3 and most of the later versions of MPICH2.

To begin the installation, ensure that the Raspberry Pi has a valid Internet connection. Run the following commands in order to get a working installation of MPICH:

1. Update your Raspbian distribution:

    ```
    sudo apt-get update
    ```

2. Create a directory to store the MPICH files:

    ```
    mkdir mpich
    cd ~/mpich
    ```

3. Get the MPICH tar file:

    ```
    wget http://www.mpich.org/static/downloads/3.2/mpich-3.2.tar.gz
    ```

4. Extract the tar archive:

    ```
    tar xfz mpich-3.2.tar.gz
    ```

5. This will contain the MPICH installation and build the following:

```
sudo mkdir /home/rpimpi/
sudo mkdir /home/rpimpi/mpi-install
mkdir /home/pi/mpi-build
cd /home/pi/mpi-build
```

6. Fortran is a dependency for MPI:

```
sudo apt-get install gfortran
```

Now, since we created a build folder for the MPICH installation earlier, we need to configure the installation script and point it to the folder where we want the interface to be installed. We do this by running the `configure` script and setting the build prefix to the installation directory:

```
sudo /home/pi/mpich/mpich-3.2/configure -prefix=/home/rpimpi/mpi-install
```

Finally, we carry out the actual installation.

```
sudo make
sudo make install
```

 Keep in mind that this build might take about an hour to complete. Make sure that the Raspberry Pi stays on for the entire period of the build.

Edit the `bashrc` file so that the path to the MPICH installation is loaded to the PATH variable every time we open a new terminal window. To do that, open the file in the terminal with the following command:

```
nano ~/.bashrc
```

Then, add the following line at the end:

```
PATH=$PATH:/home/rpimpi/mpi-install/bin
```

Save and exit the `bashrc` file by pressing *Ctrl* + *X* and then click on **Return**. We will now test the installation. For that, reboot the Pi:

```
sudo reboot
```

Then, run the following command:

```
mpiexec -n 1 hostname
```

If the preceding command returns `Pi1`, or whatever you set your hostname to be, then our MPICH installation is successful and we can proceed to the next step.

We will now look at a short C program that uses MPICH. This is given as follows:

```
#include "mpi.h"
#include <stdio.h>

void main(int argc, char *argv[]) {
    int rank, size
    MPI_Init(argc, argv);
    MPI_Comm_rank( MPI_COMM_WORLD, &rank);
    MPI_Comm_size( MPI_COMM_WORLD, &size);
    printf("I have %d rank and %d size \n", rank, size);
    MPI_Finalize();
}
```

This program runs on a single node and discovers the total number of nodes in a network. It then communicates with the MPI processes on other nodes and finds out its own rank.

The `MPI_Init()` function initiates the MPICH process on our computer according to the given information about the IP addresses in a network. The `MPI_Comm_rank()` function and the `MPI_Comm_size()` function get the rank of the current process and the total size of the network and save them in `rank` and `size` variables, respectively. The `MPI_Finalize()` function is nothing but an exit routine that ends the MPI process cleanly.

On its own, MPICH can be run using C and Fortran languages. But that might be a hindrance for a lot of users. But fret not! We can use MPICH in Python by installing the Python API called MPI4PY.

Installing MPI4PY

The conventional way of installing the `mpi4py` module from a package manager such as apt-get or aptitude does not work because it tries to install the `openMPI` library along with it, which conflicts with the existing installation of MPICH.

So, we have to install it manually. We do this by first cloning the repository from BitBucket:

```
git clone https://bitbucket.org/mpi4py/mpi4py
```

```
pi@Pi1 ~ $ git clone https://bitbucket.org/mpi4py/mpi4py
Cloning into 'mpi4py'...
remote: Counting objects: 9993, done.
remote: Compressing objects: 100% (3831/3831), done.
remote: Total 9993 (delta 6960), reused 8820 (delta 5965)
Receiving objects: 100% (9993/9993), 6.01 MiB | 100 KiB/s, done.
Resolving deltas: 100% (6960/6960), done.
pi@Pi1 ~ $
```

Make sure that all the dependencies for the library are met. These are as follows:

- Python 2.6 or higher
- A functional MPICH installation
- Cython

The first two dependencies are already met. We can install Cython with the following command:

```
sudo apt-get install cython
```

The following commands will install mpi4py with the `setup.py` installation script:

```
cd mpi4py
python setup.py build
python setup.py install
```

Add the path to the installation of mpi4py to PYTHONPATH so that the Python environment knows where the installation files are located. This ensures that we are easily able to import mpi4py into our Python applications:

```
export PYTHONPATH=/home/pi/mpi4py
```

Finally, run a test script to test the installation:

```
python demo/helloworld.py
```

Now that we have completely set up the system to use MPICH, we need to do this for every Pi we wish to use. We can run all of the earlier commands in freshly installed SD cards, but the better option would be to copy the card we prepared earlier into blank SD cards. This saves us the hassle of completely setting up the system from scratch. But remember to change the hostname to our standard scheme (such as Pi01 and Pi02) after the fresh SD card has been set up in a new Raspberry Pi. For Windows, there is an easy-to-use tool called Win32 Disk Imager, which we can use to clone the card into an `.img` file and then copy it to another blank SD card. If you are using OS X or Linux, then the following procedure should be followed:

1. Copy the OS from an existing card:

   ```
   sudo dd bs=4M if=/dev/disk2 of=~/Desktop/raspi.img
   ```

    Replace `disk2` with your own SD card

2. Remove the card and insert a new card.
3. Unmount the card.
4. Format the SD card.
5. Copy the OS to the SD card:

   ```
   sudo dd bs=4M if=~/Desktop/raspi.img of=/dev/disk2
   ```

    To know more about the mpi4py library and to have a look at the various demos, you can visit the official Git repository on BitBucket at `https://bitbucket.org/mpi4py/mpi4py`.

Setting up the Raspberry Pi cluster

Now that we have a running Raspbian distribution in all the Raspberry Pi devices that we wish to use, we will now connect them to create a cluster. We would need a networking hub that has at least the same number of LAN ports as the size of your cluster should be. For the purposes of this chapter, we will use three Raspberry Pis, so we would need a hub that has at least three LAN ports.

If you have a Wi-Fi router, then it should already have some ports at the back, as shown in the following image:

We also need three networking cables, such as those with an Ethernet connector, where one port goes into the Raspberry Pi and the other goes into the networking hub. They will look like the ones shown in the following image:

Connect one end of the Ethernet cable to the Raspberry Pi and the other end to the router for all the devices. Once we complete this networking setup, we can move on to connecting the Raspberry Pi devices with software.

Setting up SSH access from the host to the client

In the setup described here, one master node will control the other slave nodes. The master is called the host and the slaves are called clients. To access the client from the host, we use something called SSH. It is used to get the terminal access to the client from the host, and the command used is as follows:

```
ssh pi@192.168.1.5
```

Here, the preceding IP address can be replaced with the IP address of our Raspberry Pi. The IP address of a Pi can be found by simply opening up a new terminal and entering the following command:

```
ifconfig
```

This will give you the IP address associated with your connected network and the interface, which is eth0 in our case. A small problem with using this is that every time we try to SSH into a client, we need a password. To remove this restriction, we need to authorize the master to log in to the client. How we do that is by generating an RSA key from the master and then transferring it to the client. Each device has a unique RSA key, and hence, whenever a client receives an SSH request from an authorized RSA device, it will not ask for the password. To do that, we must first generate a public private key pair from the master, which is done using a command in the following format:

```
ssh-keygen -t rsa -C "your_email@youremail.com"
```

It will look something like this:

```
pi@Pi1 ~ $ ssh-keygen -t rsa -C "arushk1@gmail.com"
Generating public/private rsa key pair.
Enter file in which to save the key (/home/pi/.ssh/id_rsa):
Created directory '/home/pi/.ssh'.
Enter passphrase (empty for no passphrase):
Enter same passphrase again:
Your identification has been saved in /home/pi/.ssh/id_rsa.
Your public key has been saved in /home/pi/.ssh/id_rsa.pub.
The key fingerprint is:
41:68:30:de:fb:78:ec:df:5e:ed:1c:0a:ec:86:de:ba arushk1@gmail.com
The key's randomart image is:
+--[ RSA 2048]----+
|      o. ..      |
|     . oo.       |
|     ... .       |
|       . .       |
|      . S        |
|       +  .      |
|     . + .o    . |
|      o .oo...o. |
|       oE=+o.  o |
+-----------------+
pi@Pi1 ~ $
```

To transfer this key into the slave Raspberry Pis, we need to know each of their IP addresses. This is easily done by logging into their Pi and entering `ifconfig`.

Next, we need to copy our keys to the slave Raspberry Pi. This is done by the following command, replacing the given IP address with the IP address of your own Raspberry Pi:

```
cat ~/.ssh/id_rsa.pub | ssh pi@192.168.1.5 "mkdir .ssh;cat >> .ssh/
authorized_keys"
```

Now that we have copied our keys to the slave Raspberry Pi, we should be able to log in without a password with the standard SSH command:

```
ssh pi@192.168.1.5
```

Running code in parallel

We have now successfully completed the prerequisites for the running of code on multiple machines. We will now learn how to run our code on the Raspberry Pi cluster using the MPICH library. We will first run a demo included with the `mpi4py` module, and then we will run an N-Body simulation on our cluster. Sounds fun? Let's get into it.

First, we need to tell the MPICH library the IP address of each of the Pis in our network. This is done by simply creating a new file called `machinefile` in the home folder, which contains a list of the IP addresses of all the Raspberry Pis connected to our network. Execute the following command to create the file:

```
nano machinefile
```

Then, add the IP address of each Raspberry Pi in a new line so that the final result looks like this:

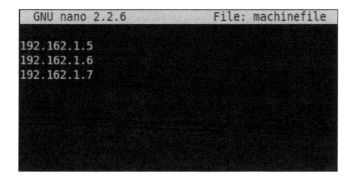

Note that we have added three IP addresses because two Raspberry Pis are slaves and one is a master. So, the MPICH library knows that it needs to run the code on these three devices. Also, note that MPICH does not differentiate between devices. It just needs a valid installation of the library to run properly. This means that we can add different versions of Raspberry Pi to our cluster or even other computers such as a BeagleBone, which has a valid installation of MPICH.

To test our setup, we navigate to the `mpi4py/demo` directory with the following command:

```
cd ~/mpi4py/demo
```

Then, we run the following command:

```
mpiexec -f ~/machinefile -n 3 python helloworld.py
```

It will give an output similar to this:

```
Hello, World! I am process 1 of 3 on Pi1.
Hello, World! I am process 2 of 3 on Pi2.
Hello, World! I am process 3 of 3 on Pi3.
```

Performance benchmarking of the cluster

Since we have successfully created a cluster of Raspberry Pis, we now need to test their performance. One way of doing that is to measure the latency between different nodes. To this end, Ohio State University has created some benchmarking tests that are included with the `mpi4py` library. We will run a few of these to measure the performance of our cluster. Simply put, latency measures the amount of time a packet takes to reach its destination and get a response. The lower the latency, the better a cluster will perform. The tests are given in the demo folder of the `mpi4py` directory. These run in this fashion: the `osu_bcast` benchmark measures the latency of the `MPI_Bcast` collective operation across N processes. It measures the minimum, maximum, and average latency for various message lengths and over a large number of iterations.

To run the `osu_allgather.py` test, we execute the following command:

```
mpiexec -f machinefile -n 3 python osu_allgather.py
```

As an interesting experiment, try to gather the latency variation with different sizes of data. It should give you a unique insight into the functioning of the network.

Introducing N-Body simulations

An N-Body simulation is a simulation of a dynamic system of particles that are under the influence of physical forces, such as gravity or magnetism. It is mostly used in astrophysics to study the processes involving nonlinear structure formation, such as the formation of galaxies, planets, and suns. They are also used to study the evolution of the large-scale structure of the universe, including estimating the dynamics of a few body systems such as the earth, moon, and sun.

Now, N-body simulations require a lot of computational resources. For example, a 10-body system has 10*9 forces that need to be computed at the same time. You can see that, if we increase the number of particles, the number of forces increases exponentially. So a 100-body system will require 9,900 forces to be calculated simultaneously. That is why N-Body simulations are generally run on powerful computers. However, we are going to use our Raspberry Pi cluster to accomplish this task because it has three times the computational power of a single Raspberry Pi. For this task, we will use an open source library called **GalaxSee**.

GalaxSee is modeled as discrete bodies interacting through gravity. The acceleration of an object is given by the sum of the forces acting on that object, divided by its mass. If you know the acceleration of a body, you can calculate the change in velocity, and if you know the velocity, you can calculate the change in the position. Consequently, you will have the position of each object at every point of time. The more objects you have, the more forces you will need to calculate, and every object must know about every other object. To reduce the computational load on a single processor, the Galaxy code is an implementation of simple parallelism. The most computationally heavy calculations involve calculating the forces on a single object, and hence, each client is involved with that calculation given the object's information and the information about each object that exerts force on it. The master then collects the computed forces from the clients.

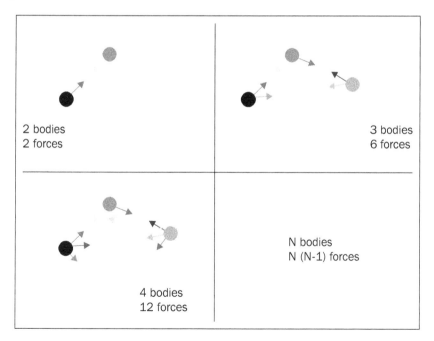

In this way, we can simulate an N-Body simulation with code running in parallel. Next, we will see how to install and get GalaxSee running.

To learn more about the GalaxSee library, visit
`https://www.shodor.org/master/galaxsee/`.

Installing and running GalaxSee

Now that we have a basic idea of what an N-Body simulation is and how different bodies interact with each other, we will proceed to the installation of the GalaxSee library.

First, we need to download the archive of the source code. We can do this with the `wget` command:

```
wget http://www.shodor.org/refdesk/Resources/Tutorials/MPIExamples/Gal.tgz
```

Next, we extract the `.tgz` archive, assuming it was downloaded to the home folder. If the path is different, we need to enter the correct path:

```
tar -xvzf ~/Gal.tgz
```

Navigate to the folder:

```
cd Gal
```

We need to use `Makefile` to successfully build GalaxSee on our Raspberry Pi. To do that, open the file in the terminal:

```
nano Makefile
```

Then, change the line:

```
cc = mpicc
```

to:

```
cc = mpic++
```

This is done so that the final result looks like this:

```
  GNU nano 2.2.6                                          File: Makefile


CC         = mpic++

LIBS       = -lX11 -lm

CFLAGS     = -I/opt/mpich/include
LDFLAGS    = -L/usr/X11R6/lib -L/opt/mpich/lib $(LIBS)

PROGRAM    = GalaxSee                    # name of the binary
SRCS       = Gal.cpp derivs.cpp diffeq.cpp modeldata.cpp point.cpp derivs_client.cpp
OBJS       = $(SRCS:.cpp=.o)             # object file

.SUFFIXES: .c .o

.cpp.o:
        $(CC) -c $(CFLAGS) $<

default: all

all: $(PROGRAM)

$(PROGRAM): $(OBJS)
        $(CC) -o $(PROGRAM) $(SRCS) $(CFLAGS) $(LDFLAGS)

clean:
        /bin/rm -f $(OBJS) $(PROGRAM)
```

To build the program, simply run this:

`make`

Now if you enter `ls` inside the `Gal` folder, you will see a newly created executable file named `GalaxSee`. Run the file with the following command:

`./GalaxSee`

This will execute the program and will open a new window that looks like the following:

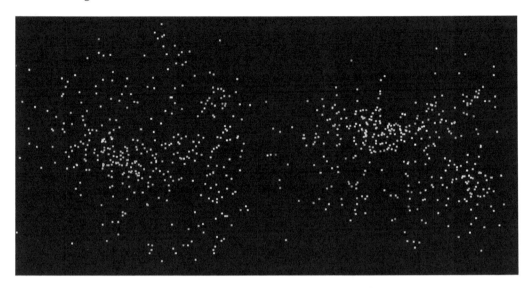

Here, the white dots are the bodies that are interacting with each other with the force of gravity. There are a few options that you can configure in GalaxSee to change the number of bodies or their interaction. For example, run the following command:

```
./GalaxSee 200 400 10000
```

Here, the first argument to the program, `200`, gives the number of bodies to be simulated. The second argument gives the speed of the simulation. The higher the number, the higher the speed. The third argument gives the amount of time to run the simulation in milliseconds. So, in the preceding command, we will simulate 200 bodies for 10 seconds. Obviously, we can experiment with different variables and see how these variables affect the simulation.

The preceding example was running on a single Raspberry Pi. But as promised, we will now see how to run it on a cluster. It will probably be surprising if we learn that the program can run on a cluster of Raspberry Pi devices with a single command and one that we've seen before. The following command does the trick:

```
mpiexec -f ~/machinefile -n 3 ./GalaxSee
```

In the preceding command, `mpiexec` initiates the MPI process on our host computer. Here, we will give it three points of data on which to execute the GalaxSee program. These are as follows:

- The path to the file containing the IP addresses for each device in the network

- The number of devices to be used

- The path to the executable file

The `-f` option specifies the machinefile. The `-n` option specifies the number of devices to be used, and finally, we give the `GalaxSee` executable file to it.

Try it for yourself! If you try to increase the number of bodies in the simulation on a single Raspberry Pi, it would probably run slower. But if you try the same on a cluster, it will definitely run faster because now, we have a lot more computational resources at our disposal.

Summary

This chapter was unique in the sense that we learned how to execute software not on a single Raspberry Pi but on multiple ones. We learned the advantages of using parallel computation and learned how to build our own network of clustered Raspberry Pi devices. We also learned how to install the libraries required for parallel computations so that we can run our own software in the cluster. We learned how to configure the Raspberry Pis in our network to communicate with each other and make the communication hassle-free. Once we set up a system, we tested it to to measure the response in the form of latency.

Finally, we learned about the concept of N-body simulation and configured an open source program to simulate it. W also saw how increasing the number of bodies in the simulation could affect the speed of the program's execution.

In the next chapter, we will expand upon this knowledge about clusters and learn about advanced networking concepts, such as DNS and DHCP. We will learn how to add functionalities such as a domain name service and auto detection of nodes and how to initiate a remote shutdown of the cluster.

12

Advanced Networking with Raspberry Pi

In the previous chapter, we built a cluster of Raspberry Pis that all interact with each other on a common network to accomplish a single task at a much greater speed than a single Raspberry Pi would perform. In fact, the MPI library is basically a networking library that delegates some computations to other processors connected in a network so that the master node doesn't have to deal with them. Now, in this chapter, we will learn about special networking concepts that power them kinds of cluster computers and in fact, the whole Internet. In this chapter, we will learn about:

- Adding DHCP capabilities to our cluster
- Adding a domain name system capability to our cluster
- Writing a script for the autodetection of nodes
- Writing scripts for the remote shutdown of cluster nodes

Introducing DHCP

DHCP (Dynamic Host Configuration Protocol): The host is simply a server, which means that the host computer is responsible for providing a service. The service could be of any kind. For example, a web server is responsible for hosting the files required for viewing a website. Again, the server implements the necessary communication protocols to allow many players to play against each other. A computer or application that uses the services offered by a server is called a client. Now you might know that every computer on the Internet is identified by a unique address known as the IP address.

A DHCP server is responsible for allocating such IP addresses to all the nodes in a network, and keeping track of the allocated addresses. In DHCP, dynamic means constantly changing, host means server, configuration refers to configuring your network settings, and protocol means a set of rules on how to do things. Described next is the procedure for the allocation of IP addresses by a DHCP server.

Suppose a node wants to join a network. It first sends a message to the server asking to be allocated an IP address. The server sends a message with an IP address and a time duration for which the node might keep that IP address. Then the server notes down the IP address given to the node in a table, along with the time it was given at and the validity duration.

Now, when the node joins a network, it has no way of knowing if there is a DHCP server. So it sends out a broadcast signal to the whole network intended just for the DHCP server. If there is a server, it sends out a reply offering an address.

Now, consider the situation when a node is shutting down or leaving the network cleanly. It sends out a signal to the server identifying itself and offers the IP address back to the DHCP server. The server then modifies the table, strikes off the host's name from the IP address, and then marks it available for allocation to other nodes in the network. But what if the node doesn't exit cleanly? For example, when the machine loses power or the network cable is just yanked out of it. This is where the time duration of allocation comes in handy. Once the duration of allocation of that IP address has passed, the node is automatically struck off from the table and that address becomes available again. Every time the server receives a packet of data from the host, its duration of allocation is automatically refreshed.

A few networking concepts

Since we have learned how a DHCP server operates, we will now work through an introduction to some important concepts related to networking that might be useful in understanding the operation of the network and also for debugging any errors we may encounter.

Though it might not look like it on first read, an IP address follows a predefined set of conventions and it is not handed out randomly. The IP address that is visible, for example `192.168.1.10`, is actually composed of binary numbers. Each number separated by a decimal is actually a binary octet. So the preceding IP address actually looks like the following:

```
11000000 10101000 00000001 00001010
```

Now, an IP address is classified into multiple classes according to the address allocated to it by the DHCP server. They serve as a hierarchical system and also help to segment the IP address into classes such as private address and external address. They also help in distributing the IP address ranges to entities such as countries, service providers, and so on. There are the following classes of IP addresses:

- Class A: In this class, the first bit of the first octet is always set to zero. So, the first octet ranges from `00000000` – `01111111`, or `0` – `127`.

  So Class A can only have an IP address from `1.X.X.X` – `126.X.X.X` as `127.0.0.1` is reserved for loopback IP addresses, that is, for the machine to refer to itself. Hence, this class can only have 126 networks (2^7 – 2) and 16777214 (2^24 -2) hosts.

- Class B: Here, the first two bits of the first are set to `1` and `0` respectively. So, the first octet ranges from `10000000` – `10111111` or, `128` – `191`.

  So, Class B can only have IP addresses ranging from `128.0.X.X` – `191.255.X.X`. Hence, this class can have 16,384 (2^14) networks and 65,534 (2^16 – 2) hosts.

- Class C: The first three bits of the first octet are set to 110. The range of the first octet is from `11000000` – `11011111`, or `192` – `223`. So, Class C can have IP addresses ranging from `192.0.0.X` – `234.255.255.X`. This means that Class C has a total of 20,97,152 (2^21) networks and 254 (2^8 -2) host addresses.

- Class D: This class of network has the first four bits of the first octet set as `1110`. That gives it a range of `11100000` – `11101111` or `235` – `239`. However, unlike the preceding three classes, Class D is used exclusively for multicasting. So, there is no need to get individual IP addresses, because individual host data is not required for this network to operate.

- Class E: This class is reserved exclusively use for experiments, or R&D, or study. The IP addresses in this class can range from `240.0.0.0` – `255.255.255.254`.

Now, we move on to the concept of a subnet mask. A subnet mask is basically a 32-bit address that divides an IP address into the network and host addresses. A subnet mask sets all the bits for the network as 1 and all the bits for the host as 0. So, the subnet masks for the different classes of networks are given as follows:

- Class A: `255.0.0.0`
- Class B: `255.255.0.0`
- Class C: `255.255.255.0`

Class D and Class E do not have subnet addresses because Class D has multicast addresses and Class E only consists of reserved addresses.

Configuring a Raspberry Pi to act as a DHCP server

Now, we will perform a hands-on implementation of the preceding concept by setting up a Raspberry Pi from our cluster to act as the DHCP server. The Raspberry Pi selected for the purpose should be properly marked for identification because there can be only one DHCP server in a network. More than one can cause a lot of problems! If we have more than one DHCP server in a single network, the client nodes will get confused as to which server to send the IP allocation request to. We first need to install a program called dnsmasq, and we can do that with the following commands:

```
sudo apt-get update
sudo apt-get install dnsmasq
```

Once this is installed, we can go ahead and disconnect the Internet from the LAN and connect the network to a non-DHCP hub. Why, you may ask? Because the conventional routers that we use have a DHCP server built into them. So configuring a Raspberry Pi as a server and connecting it to the router might cause some problems. So we just connect it to a networking hub that interconnects all the nodes. We are now ready to modify the Raspberry Pi to get it running as a server.

By convention, DHCP servers will have the lowest IP address in a network from the range of IP addresses. And for a lot of private networks, this IP address space looks like this: `192.168.0.X`. This means that the DHCP server will generally have `192.168.0.1` as the IP address and the other nodes will have `192.168.0.2, 3, 4`, and so on up to 254 IP addresses.

So, logically, we need our Raspberry Pi to have this address and hold on to it so it defaults to the DHCP server every time the network is initiated. So, edit the network interfaces file:

```
sudo nano /etc/network/interfaces
```

In the interfaces file, `eth0` refers to the connection from the `ethernet` port. If you've connected a Wi-Fi dongle to it, you will also see a `wlan0` interface. This translates to `Wireless LAN 0`. Now, since our Pi is connected via an `ethernet` port, we find the following statement:

```
iface eth0 inet dhcp
```

Basically, this line is the one responsible for the Raspberry Pi acting as a DHCP client because it tells the Pi to try to get an IP address from a DHCP server, from the interface `eth0`. But since we want our Raspberry Pi to act as a DHCP server in the network, we comment this line out. Then, to set a static IP address for our server, we add the following lines:

```
# iface eth0 inet dhcp
auto eth0
iface eth0 inet static
address 192.168.1.1
netmask 255.255.255.0
```

The `interfaces` file might look something like:

```
GNU nano 2.2.6          File: /etc/network/interfaces

auto lo
iface lo inet loopback

auto eth0
iface eth0 inet static
address 192.168.1.1
netmask 255.255.255.0
```

The **static** option tells the Raspberry Pi to configure a static IP address and **netmask**, which is given in the statement below. Now, save this file by pressing *Ctrl + X* and *Enter*. To restart the networking service, enter the following command:

```
sudo service networking restart
```

Now, the Raspberry Pi's IP address will always be set to **192.168.1.1**. We can also check this, as we did previously, by entering the command:

```
ifconfig
```

Now, we need to set up the software we installed earlier: dnsmasq. This is nothing but a DHCP server application for which we need to manually specify a configuration file according to our preferences. But since there already exists a default configuration file, we will make a backup of it. To do that, enter the following commands:

```
cd /etc
sudo mv dnsmasq.conf dnsmasq.default
```

The following command creates a new configuration file for dnsmasq:

```
sudo nano dnsmasq.conf
```

Once in the editing screen, enter the following lines into the configuration file:

```
interface=eth0
dhcp-range=192.168.1.2,192.168.1.254,255.255.255.0,12h
```

The first line in the file specifies the interface on which to listen to incoming DHCP requests. In this case, we have set it up to be the ethernet port of the Pi. The dhcp-range takes in four parameters:

- Lowest IP address to be allotted
- Highest IP address to be allotted
- Netmask
- Lease duration

We can now save and close the file by pressing *Ctrl* + *X* and *Enter*. For the settings to take effect, we need to ensure that our DHCP serves the Raspberry Pi and is the only device connected to the networking hub. Once all the other devices are removed, we can restart the DHCP service by:

```
sudo service dnsmasq restart
```

The DHCP server is now running and can listen to requests from clients connected to the same networking hub.

Finally, ensure that none of the other Raspberry Pis have a static IP address that is in conflict with our DHCP server. Preferably, there should not be any Pi with a static IP configured. The `/etc/network/interfaces` file should be as follows:

```
iface eth0 inet dhcp
# auto eth0
# iface eth0 inet static
# address 192.168.0.1
# netmask 255.255.255.0
```

Exit nano and restart the networking service with the following command:

```
sudo service networking restart
```

Now, we can connect all the Client Raspberry Pis to the networking hub. Once they are all switched on, they should be able to acquire their respective IP addresses from the DHCP server immediately. We can also check the allocated IP addresses by running the `ifconfig` command on the clients. The IP addresses are allocated randomly from the range given to the DHCP server.

Once the IP addresses are acquired, everything should work as expected. We can check the connections by pinging different nodes from another node. Do this with the following command:

```
ping 192.168.1.X
```

where X is the IP address of the other node. We can also check the connection to the DHCP server with:

```
ping 192.168.1.1
```

Another interesting experiment that can be performed with the setup is actually observing the connections go up and down. Firstly, we can shut down a client and observe it give back the IP address to the server. Run the following on a client of your selection:

```
sudo ifdown eth0
```

Once we do that, we will see an output similar to the following:

```
Listening on LPF/eth0/b8:27:eb:a8:6b:cc
Sending on   LPF/eth0/b8:27:eb:a8:6b:cc
Sending on   Socket/fallback
DHCPRELEASE on eth0 to 192.168.1.1 port 67
```

DHCPRELEASE is the actual statement where the IP address is handed back to the server by the client. Similarly, we restart the eth0 and observe the DHCP address being acquired. Run the following command:

```
sudo ifup eth0
```

We will see an output similar to the following:

```
Listening on LPF/eth0/b8:27:eb:a8:6b:cc

Sending on    LPF/eth0/b8:27:eb:a8:6b:cc

Sending on    Socket/fallback

DHCPDISCOVER on eth0 to 255.255.255.255 port 67 interval 7
DHCPREQUEST on eth0 to 255.255.255.255 port 67

DHCPOFFER from 192.168.1.1

DHCPACK from 192.168.1.1
bound to 192.168.0.X -- renewal in 40000 seconds
```

In this exchange, DCHPDISCOVER, DHCPREQUEST, DHCPOFFER, and DHCPACK are of importance. They correlate with the acquisition procedure in the IP address through a DHCP server, as described before. It is left as an exercise to the reader to figure out their respective functions.

Introducing Domain Naming System (DNS)

In the previous section, we learned to add the DHCP server to our Raspberry Pi cluster. This was done mainly so that each Raspberry Pi in our cluster could be identified by a unique IP address. Now, as you can imagine, the bigger our cluster grows, the harder it is going to be to remember the IP address of each Raspberry Pi. Humans find it hard to remember long sequences of numbers, which is what the IP addresses are. But there is a way by which we can easily connect to different nodes without having to remember their IP addresses.

This method is called a **Domain Name System (DNS)**. Its basic function is to translate IP addresses into words so that it becomes easier for us to remember. For example, the DNS server will translate the IP address 192.168.5.43 into raspberrypi.org and vice versa to make it easier to connect to. Indeed, this is what happens on the Internet. Each website has an IP address behind it.

When you type a URL into your browser, your computer first contacts the DNS server and asks for the IP address that it is associated with. The DNS server then searches its database for the name and returns the IP address to your computer. This whole process is called a DNS query.

Now, we can have multiple DNS servers in a single network. This way, when one DNS server doesn't have an address saved in its database, it can pass the query to the second DNS server, and so on. This is known as an iterative DNS query. This is what actually happens on the Internet. There are millions of websites on the Internet and having a single DNS server that holds a large database is not only unfeasible but also unreliable. So, there are millions of DNS servers that are distributed across the world and act together to resolve billions of translation requests from millions of clients.

 But here is an interesting problem. In a DHCP network, IP addresses are dynamic, which means that the IP address of a node might change. Think about how a DNS server might handle that situation. You can do that as an exercise.

Setting up a DNS server on the Pi

Now, we will learn about the practical part of setting up a Domain Name System server on our own cluster of Raspberry Pis so as to learn the intricacies of the system. We will set up a DNS server on the same Pi on which we set up the DHCP server earlier. Since we took care to see that it is easily identifiable from the other client Raspberry Pis, we can begin the setting-up procedure.

We use the same software, dnsmasq, which we used for the DHCP server, as it also has the capability to run a DNS server. Other than that, we don't need to install anything extra. As a sanity check, before beginning the following tutorial, try to ping the server from one of the clients. Although multiple DNS servers can be configured, for the purposes of this tutorial, we will be using only one Raspberry Pi as the server.

As the DNS server doesn't have a broadcast system like DHCP, the clients can't locate it easily. So they need to be told the IP address of the DNS server, and one way of doing it is to make the DHCP server pass the IP address to the client. This can be done at the same time as the DHCP server is allotting its own IP address. In this case, the IP address of both the DHCP server and the DNS server is the same. Open up the dnsmasq configuration file (dnsmasq.conf) for editing with the following command:

```
sudo nano /etc/dnsmasq.conf
```

The first thing we do is specify that the IP address of the DNS server and DHCP server is the same. To do this, add the following line at the end of the file:

```
dhcp-option=6,192.168.1.1
```

Now that the clients know where the DNS server is located, we need to create a lookup database that contains the IP addresses with their corresponding names. Although in actual DNS servers a more sophisticated database platform is used, for example SQL, here we will use a simple text file as a demonstration. Add the following two lines to the configuration file:

```
no-hosts
addn-hosts=/etc/hosts.dnsmasq
```

Here, the `no-hosts` line tells `dnsmasq` to ignore the default `/etc/hosts` file for DNS queries. And the next line specifies that our own file, `/etc/hosts.dnsmasq`, should be used for DNS queries.

The next step in this process is to create our hosts file. To do that, enter the following command:

```
sudo nano /etc/hosts.dnsmasq
```

Since this file that didn't exist before, we should now be editing a blank file. New entries can be added in a specific format, which is the IP Address, followed by a tab, followed by the name. For example:

```
192.168.1.1    server
```

Here, the first part is the IP address, the second part is the tab spacing, and the third part is the name associated with that IP address.

 We have to add a tab instead of multiple spaces for it to work.

Now, save and exit this file. Make sure that the server is the only device connected to the networking switch. Unplug all other devices before restarting the `dnsmasq` service. Restart the service with the following command:

```
sudo service dnsmasq restart
```

But there is one more thing. Since our server is set up with a static IP address, we also need to tell the DHCP server to use its own DNS server. We do that through a file named `/etc/resolv.conf`. Open it for editing by:

```
sudo nano /etc/resolve.conf
```

Change the contents of the file to:

```
nameserver 127.0.0.1
```

Now, `127.0.0.1` is a reserved IP address that is used to refer to one's own system. So, it would be the same if we put `192.168.1.1` as the IP address. However, if the server's IP address changes, we would need to change this file manually. So, we put 127.0.0.1 as the IP address of the nameserver. Exit the file and restart the networking service:

```
sudo service networking restart
```

Finally, connect all the client Raspberry Pis to the networking hub. They should start receiving their allocated IP addresses. Once all the Pis are connected to the network, you can run:

```
ping server
```

And you will start getting a response. If this is successful, it means that the ping request was first passed to the DNS server inside the server Pi and, when the hostname was resolved, a response was obtained from the IP address of the server.

Configuring the setup for a web server

Let's say, for example, one of the Raspberry Pis is configured as a web server. So, the task now will be to set up the cluster in such a way that you can type a name in a browser and have the home page of the web server load up!

By convention, web servers are supposed to have static IP addresses. This is so that DNS servers can store their hostnames without worrying too much about IP addresses changing. Since we earlier put in the entire range of IP addresses possible as the range for the DHCP server, we will modify that range so that we can reserve some static IP addresses for our web servers. For this, again edit the `/etc/dnsmasq.conf` file and modify the `dhcp-range` variable to the following:

```
dhcp-range=192.168.1.40,192.168.1.254,255.255.255.0,12h
```

So, now we have non-DHCP IP addresses from 192.168.1.2 to 192.168.1.39, which we can allot to the web servers. One of the ways to do this is to modify `/etc/network/interfaces` and `/etc/resolve.conf` on the web server itself and set it so that the web server always gets a static IP address. But, we can also identify the web server by its MAC address, which is the unique hardware address of the network interface, and give it the same IP address every time.

This would require a modification of the `dnsmasq.conf` file. We need to know the MAC address of our web server Pi for this. It can be easily found by executing `ifconfig` in a new terminal and looking for the `HWaddr` field ; it will be in the form `b8:27:eb:a8:6b:cc`. Remember that this address is unique for every device. Once we have this address, we will add the following line in the `dnsmasq.conf` file on the server Pi to assign a specific IP address for this MAC address:

```
dhcp-host=b8:27:eb:a8:6b:cc,192.168.1.5
```

This configures the DHCP server to always allot the `192.168.1.5` IP address for this MAC address. Now, we just need to add a name for our web server in the `hosts.dnsconf` file. Open it for editing with `nano` and just add the following line at the end of the file:

```
192.168.1.5   webserver
```

So, it finally looks like this:

Restart the `dnsmasq` service for the changes to take effect by:

```
sudo service dnsmasq restart
```

Finally, we have to make the web server Pi take up the new IP address so that it can be addressed by name in the DNS server. To do this, execute the following commands:

```
sudo ifdown eth0
```

```
sudo ifup eth0
```

This will make the Raspberry Pi disengage with the DHCP server; when it tries to re-acquire the IP address, the DHCP server will allot the static IP address we defined in the configuration file.

To test if the DNS server works with the web server or not, you can run the following command from any of the other client Pis:

```
ping webserver
```

If you get a response, it means a DNS server is set up correctly. If not, then you need to check whether all the steps were followed correctly.

Automating node discovery in a network

Currently, we have very few devices in our network. But, there will be a situation when there will be many nodes and managing them manually will be a difficult task. In a large cluster, there will be many nodes that are inactive or unserviceable. If we try to connect to them using a script that has the IP address of the clients hardcoded, we will meet with a lot of errors. This is why there is a need for automatic node detection that automatically detects the active nodes in a network and saves that information so that other programs can use it. One such program is MPICH, which we learned about in the previous chapter. As you might have learned, whenever we execute a program using MPICH, we have specified a filename that contains a list of active nodes that can be used for computations. However, if one of the nodes is inactive or unresponsive, the script will not work properly and will waste valuable computation resources.

For node discovery in a network, we will use a program called Nmap, which is short for network map. Nmap is a free security scanner, port discovery, and network exploration tool. Install it using the following command:

```
sudo apt-get install nmap
```

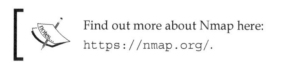
Find out more about Nmap here:
`https://nmap.org/`.

As we learned with the IP addresses in the second section, the following IP address:

```
192.168.1.1
```

actually looks like the following:

```
11000000 10101000 00000001 00000001
```

Now that we have this information, we can move on to learn how to use the Nmap tool. The commands for scanning active IP addresses are:

```
nmap -sP 192.168.1.0/24
nmap -sP 192.168.1.5-100
```

This is what the output looks like:

```
pi@Pi1: ~ 80x24
pi@Pi1 ~ $ nmap -sP 192.168.1.1/24

Starting Nmap 6.00 ( http://nmap.org ) at 2015-12-09 01:39 UTC
Nmap scan report for 192.168.1.1
Host is up (0.014s latency).
Nmap scan report for Pi1.lan (192.168.1.79)
Host is up (0.0026s latency).
Nmap scan report for              (192.168.1.147)
Host is up (0.062s latency).
Nmap scan report for              (192.168.1.151)
Host is up (0.0098s latency).
Nmap done: 256 IP addresses (4 hosts up) scanned in 2.58 seconds
pi@Pi1 ~ $
```

The preceding are two separate commands and we will learn what each of them does. The first command scans the whole range of IP addresses in a network from `192.168.1.0` – `192.168.1.255`. In this command, we specify a mask of 24 bits, which basically tells Nmap to not change the first 24 bits of the IP address, which, according to the information we learned earlier, means that the first three numbers of the IP address will remain constant and only the last number will be varied and checked for a response. Since our network will only contain IP addresses starting with `192.168.1`, due to the way our DHCP server is set up, this approach is good.

The second command explicitly specifies the range of the IP addresses to scan. This is useful as you want to find active nodes in a specific range. One use case for this is to find out all the client nodes in a network.

Summary

In this chapter, we built upon the foundations laid down in the previous chapter to gain more understanding about the concepts of networking and how they are applied to a cluster of Raspberry Pis.

Specifically, we learned how to set up a DHCP server on a Raspberry Pi and learned the mechanics of how IP addresses are allocated to different clients. We also observed the exact procedure of how the allocation takes place.

As a next step, we set up a DNS server, too, that works with the DHCP server and assigns names to the IP addresses so that the nodes are easily accessible. Using the same methodology, we learned how to assign a name for a Raspberry Pi-based web server so that we can open websites on our own network.

Finally, we learned about a tool that helps us discover active nodes on the network so that we do not have to face the inconvenience of assigning computations to a non-active node that could potentially crash a program or wrong computations.

13
Setting Up a Web Server on the Raspberry Pi

In the previous two chapters, we discussed the networking capabilities of the Raspberry Pi. In *Chapter 11, Build Your Own Supercomputer with Raspberry Pi*, we built a network of Raspberry Pi devices that were able to communicate with each other and share the computational burden, thereby significantly reducing the time required for a task to complete. In the next chapter, *Chapter 12, Advanced Networking with Raspberry Pi*, we learned about more advanced networking concepts such as DHCP servers, DNS systems, and so on. In addition to that, we made our own intranet with a few Pi devices.

Continuing the same theme, we will now set up a web server on a single Raspberry Pi and set up a WordPress installation on it. The web server that we will be using is Apache, as it is one of the most popular servers, and has high usage within the open source community. In this chapter, we will be covering the following topics:

- Introducing and installing Apache
- Learning to serve HTML websites
- Installing PHP and MySQL
- Installing WordPress
- Configuring WordPress

Introducing and installing Apache on Raspbian

The Apache HTTP server is extremely popular and is the world's most used web server software currently. It enjoys the support of the open source community because it is developed and maintained by an open community of developers under the umbrella of the Apache Software Foundation. Although most commonly used on a Unix-like system, it is available for a variety of other operating systems including Microsoft Windows. In 2009, it became the first web server to be used by more than a hundred million websites and currently it is estimated to serve over 50 percent of all websites and 37 percent of the top servers across domains.

One of the reasons it is so popular is that it supports a wide variety of features and many more features can be implemented as compiled modules that can extend the core functionality. For example, on its own, Apache can serve HTML files over HTTP, but with additional modules installed, it can also serve web pages using languages such as Python. It also has a variety of language interfaces that include Python, PHP, and Perl.

Now, installing the web server on a Raspbian distribution is extremely easy. We need to install the `apache2` package with the following command:

```
$ sudo apt-get install apache2
```

During installation, the package automatically creates our demo HTML file that you can see if you type `127.0.0.1` or `http://localhost/` on your URL bar. We can also see this if we navigate to the Pi's IP address from another machine connected to the same network such as `192.168.1.5`. Replace this IP address with your own Pi's IP address in the network. You can find the IP address by typing the following on the Raspberry Pi's terminal:

```
$ hostname -I
```

The default page looks like this:

Apache2 Ubuntu Default Page

It works!

This is the default welcome page used to test the correct operation of the Apache2 server after installation on Ubuntu systems. It is based on the equivalent page on Debian, from which the Ubuntu Apache packaging is derived. If you can read this page, it means that the Apache HTTP server installed at this site is working properly. You should **replace this file** (located at /var/www/html/index.html) before continuing to operate your HTTP server.

If you are a normal user of this web site and don't know what this page is about, this probably means that the site is currently unavailable due to maintenance. If the problem persists, please contact the site's administrator.

Configuration Overview

Ubuntu's Apache2 default configuration is different from the upstream default configuration, and split into several files optimized for interaction with Ubuntu tools. The configuration system is **fully documented in /usr/share/doc/apache2/README.Debian.gz**. Refer to this for the full documentation. Documentation for the web server itself can be found by accessing the **manual** if the apache2-doc package was installed on this server.

The configuration layout for an Apache2 web server installation on Ubuntu systems is as follows:

```
/etc/apache2/
|-- apache2.conf
|       `--  ports.conf
|-- mods-enabled
|       |-- *.load
|       `-- *.conf
|-- conf-enabled
|       `-- *.conf
|-- sites-enabled
|       `-- *.conf
|
```

- apache2.conf is the main configuration file. It puts the pieces together by including all remaining configuration files when starting up the web server.
- ports.conf is always included from the main configuration file. It is used to determine the listening ports for

If we see this page, it means that our installation has been successful. This is just a single HTML file that can be found at /var/www/html/index.html. Let's look at the details of this folder. Navigate to the folder by:

```
$ cd /var/www/html/
```

And then execute the following command to see the properties of the files in the folder:

```
$ ls -al
```

This command lists the files and a few of their properties. You will see the following output:

```
total 20
drwxr-xr-x 2 root root  4096 Dec 11 12:13 .
drwxr-xr-x 4 root root  4096 Dec 11 12:21 ..
-rw-r--r-- 1 root root 11510 Dec 11 12:13 index.html
```

The meaning of the columns respectively is:

- Permissions of the file
- Number of files in the directory
- User that owns the file/directory
- Group that owns the file/directory
- File size
- Last modified date

Since the owner of the index.html file is root, we need to take ownership of the file before editing it. To do that, enter the following command:

```
$ sudo chown pi: index.html
```

We can also replace the index.html file with our own HTML file and serve a fully fledged HTML website complete with CSS classes.

However, a simple HTML website sounds too basic, right? Since we are on the final leg of this book, we should do something more advanced. That's right, in the following sections we will be learning how to set up a WordPress website. For that, however, we first need to install a few tools that WordPress uses.

Installing PHP and MySQL

PHP is one of the most popular programming languages in use today for the web look at. It is the code that runs on the server when it receives a request for a website. Unlike HTML, PHP can generate dynamic web pages that can change the look and content on the fly. We chose PHP to work with because WordPress uses PHP. Now, install PHP and the accompanying Apache packages with the following command:

```
$ sudo apt-get install php5 libapache2-mod-php5
```

We now have PHP installed with its accompanying Apache packages, and we will proceed to test it.

Navigate to the HTML folder and create a new `index.php` file:

```
$ cd /var/www/html/
$ sudo nano index.php
```

Add a test line to it:

```
<?php echo "hello world"; ?>
```

Save the file and exit by pressing *Ctrl* + *X* and then *Y*. We also need to remove the `index.html` file because HTML takes precedence over PHP. Do that with the following command:

```
sudo rm index.html
```

Navigate to `127.0.0.1` or `localhost` in the browser and you will be greeted by the hello world message. Let's now set up something static.

Replace the hello world line with the following:

```
<?php echo date('Y-m-d H:i:s'); ?>
```

Now that we have installed PHP to process the web pages that we want, the next step is to install a database to store some data. Our database of choice will be MySQL simply because WordPress uses it to store IDs of things such as Post, Pages, Comments, Users, and so on.

To install MySQL and its PHP packages, run the following command:

```
sudo apt-get install mysql-server php5-mysql
```

Once the installation proceeds, you will be asked for a root password for creating the databases. Enter the password and remember it for future use.

Installing WordPress

Now that we are done installing the dependencies, the next step is getting the WordPress files in the HTML folder. Fortunately for us, WordPress provides a tar archive of the latest version of WordPress on this link: `http://wordpress.org/latest.tar.gz`. We now need to place the files contained in this folder in our web server folder. To do that, we first need to take ownership of the folder. To carry out that entire process, we execute the following commands:

```
$ cd /var/www/html/
$ sudo chown pi:
$ sudo rm *
$ wget http://wordpress.org/latest.tar.gz
```

In a nutshell, we first navigate to the HTML folder, take ownership of the folder, remove all the pre-existing files, and then fetch the WordPress archive. Next, we extract the contents of the archive and place them in the HTML folder. We do that with the following commands:

```
$ tar xzf latest.tar.gz
$ mv wordpress/*
$ rm -rf wordpress latest.tar.gz
```

Now, if you run the `ls` command, you will see the following output:

```
|-- index.php
|-- license.txt
|-- readme.html
|-- wp-activate.php
|-- wp-admin
|-- wp-blog-header.php
|-- wp-comments-post.php
|-- wp-config-sample.php
|-- wp-content
|-- wp-cron.php
|-- wp-includes
|-- wp-links-opml.php
|-- wp-load.php
|-- wp-login.php
|-- wp-mail.php
|-- wp-settings.php
|-- wp-signup.php
|-- wp-trackback.php
`-- xmlrpc.php

3 directories, 16 files
```

Configuring the WordPress installation

Once the files are properly placed in the right locations, to activate the installation and start using the WordPress website, we first need to set up a MySQL database that WordPress can use. To set up the database, execute the following command:

```
$ mysql -uroot -p
```

This sets up the database so that the user is root and the -p option prompts the terminal to ask for the password. Enter the same password that you entered while installing the MySQL database. We are then greeted with a MySQL terminal that looks like this:

```
Copyright (c) 2000, 2015, Oracle and/or its affiliates. All rights reserved.

Oracle is a registered trademark of Oracle Corporation and/or its
affiliates. Other names may be trademarks of their respective
owners.

Type 'help;' or '\h' for help. Type '\c' to clear the current input statement.

mysql>
```

Once inside the terminal, execute the following statement:

```
mysql> create database wordpress;
```

You will be greeted by the following message:

```
Type 'help;' or '\h' for help. Type '\c'

mysql> create database wordpress;
Query OK, 1 row affected (0.00 sec)

mysql> Bye
```

Finally, exit the terminal by pressing *Ctrl + D*.

To complete the installation, we need to access the WordPress installation page, located on our local host. So go ahead and enter `127.0.0.1` in your browser and you will be greeted with the following page:

Welcome to WordPress. Before getting started, we need some information on the database. You will need to know the following items before proceeding.

1. Database name
2. Database username
3. Database password
4. Database host
5. Table prefix (If you want to run more than one WordPress in a single database)

We're going to use this information to create a wp-config.php file. If for any reason this automatic file creation doesn't work, don't worry. All this does is fill in the database information to a configuration file. You may also simply open **wp-config-sample.php** in a text editor, fill in your information, and save it as **wp-config.php**. Need more help? <u>We got it</u>.

In all likelihood, these items were supplied to you by your Web Host. If you don't have this information, then you will need to contact them before you can continue. If you're all ready...

Let's go!

This means that WordPress is properly configured. We now hit **Let's go!** to proceed to the next step. This takes us to the following page:

Enter all the details for the database including the password that you set earlier. Enter the details on the page as given in the preceding screenshot, and then press **Submit**. The installation wizard will give an error message that it was unable to write the wp-config.php file to the filesystem. There is no reason to panic here, because it also gives us the content of the wp-config.php file that we can use to create the file manually. The error looks like this:

So, now copy the text given in the dialog box, and open a new terminal. Create a new wp-config.php file in the HTML folder with the following commands:

```
$ cd /var/www/html
$ sudo nano wp-config.php
```

Go ahead and paste the content that was copied. We can right-click to paste or simply press *Ctrl + Shift + V*. Save and exit the file by pressing *Ctrl + X* and then *Y*. Once the file is created, go back to the browser and hit the **Run the Install** button. After processing for a few seconds, the page returns the following screen:

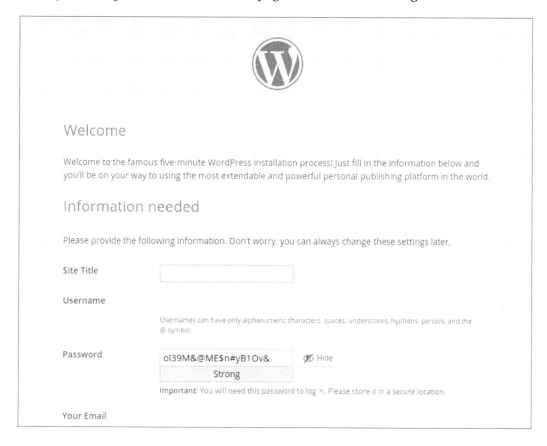

Now, we are ready to enter our details to create a user and begin using the WordPress website. Enter the details, and you've successfully created it.

You can log in to your website by appending `/wp-admin.php` to your website URL. For example, in our case the admin page will be given by `127.0.0.1/wp-admin.php`, and it looks like this:

 To find out more about WordPress, log on to their website: `https://wordpress.org/`

It would be an interesting exercise for you to continue with the process and try to run a fully fledged website on the Raspberry Pi and see how it handles the loads of running a heavy website complete with custom theme, pictures, and so on.

Summary

This chapter was a general extension of the previous two chapters, expanding on the concepts of networking built previously and using them to set up a web server on our intranet.

In this chapter, we installed the Apache web server on our Pi. To set up the WordPress website, we installed all the dependencies including PHP and MySQL. Then we downloaded the WordPress files and set up a MySQL database to work with it.

Finally, we configured the installation and resolved the errors that we generated to arrive at a complete installation.

In next chapter, we will learn network programming with Raspberry Pi using sockets in Python.

14
Network Programming in Python with the Pi

A network socket is an endpoint of a connection across computer networks. Nowadays, almost all communication between computers and distinct networks is based on the Internet Protocol, which uses sockets as a basis of communication. A socket is an abstract reference that a local program can pass to the network API to make use of a connection. Sockets are internally often represented in network programming APIs simply as integers, which identify which connection to use. In brief, we will be covering the following topics in this chapter:

- The basics of sockets
- The difference between TCP and UDP sockets
- UDP sockets
- TCP sockets
- The Telnet program
- A chat application

The basics of sockets

A socket **API** is an **application programming interface**, provided by the **operating system (OS)**, that allows application programs to initiate, control, and use network sockets programmatically for communication. Internet socket APIs are usually based on the Berkeley sockets standard. In the Berkeley sockets standard, sockets are a form of file descriptor, adhering to the Unix philosophy that *everything is a file*. Thus, we can read, write, open, and close sockets in the same way as we do files. In inter-process communications, each end will have its own socket, but these may use different socket-programming APIs. However, they are abstracted by the network protocol.

A socket address is a combination of an **Internet Protocol (IP)** address and a port number. Internet sockets deliver and receive data packets to and from the appropriate application process or thread. On a computer with an IP address, every network-related program or utility will have its own unique socket or set of sockets. This ensures that the incoming data is redirected to the correct application.

The difference between TCP and UDP

There are two types of protocols in the IP suite. They are **Transmission Control Protocol (TCP)** and **User Datagram Protocol (UDP)**. TCP is a connection-oriented IP which means that once a connection is established, data can be sent in a bidirectional manner. UDP is a much simpler, connectionless Internet protocol. Multiple messages are sent as packets in chunks using UDP. Let's distinguish between the two with clear points, as follows:

TCP	UDP
TCP is a connection-oriented protocol.	UDP is a connectionless protocol.
Using this mode, a message makes its way across the Internet from one computer and network to another. This is connection based.	UDP is also a protocol used in message transport or transfer. It is not a connection-based protocol. A program using UDP can send a lot of packets to another, and that would be the end of the relationship.
TCP is suited to applications that require high reliability, and transmission time is relatively less critical.	UDP is suitable for applications that need fast, efficient transmission, such as games and live-streaming videos.
Protocols utilizing TCP include HTTP, HTTPS, FTP, SMTP, and Telnet.	Protocols utilizing UDP include DNS, DHCP, TFTP, SNMP, RIP, and VoIP.
Data is read as a stream of bytes; no distinguishing indications are transmitted to signal message segment boundaries.	Packets are sent individually and are checked for integrity only on arrival. Packets have headers and endpoints.
TCP performs error checking.	UDP performs error checking. However, it has no recovery options for missed or corrupt packets.
The data transferred remains intact and arrives in the same order (known as in-order) in which it was sent.	There is no guarantee that the messages or packets sent will reach at all or will be in the same order as transmitted.

The architecture and programming of UDP sockets

Here is the architecture of a UDP client-server system:

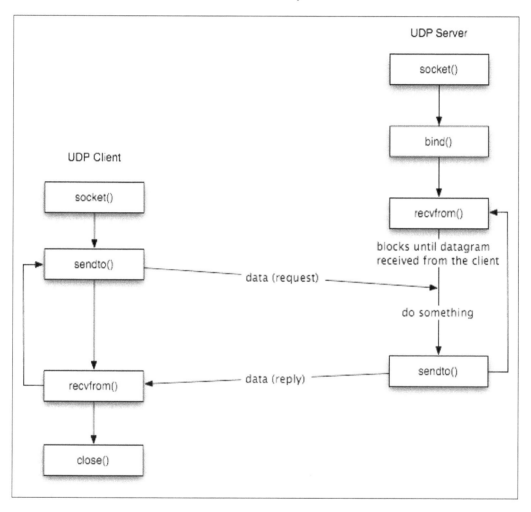

UDP is an Internet protocol. Just like its counterpart TCP (which we will discuss soon), UDP is a protocol for the transfer of packets from one host to another. However, as seen in the diagram, it has some important differences from TCP. Unlike TCP, UDP is connectionless and is not a stream-oriented protocol. This means a UDP server just catches incoming packets from any and many hosts without establishing a reliable and dedicated connection for the transfer of data between processes.

A UDP socket is created as follows in Python:

```
s = socket.socket(socket.AF_INET, socket.SOCK_DGRAM)
```

SOCK_DGRAM specifies a UDP socket.

Sending and receiving data with UDP

As UDP sockets are connectionless sockets, communication is done with the socket functions sendto() and recvfrom(). These functions do not require a socket to be connected to another peer explicitly. They just send and receive directly to and from a given IP address.

UDP servers and NCAT

The simplest form of a UDP server in Python is as follows:

```
import socket
port = 5000
s = socket.socket(socket.AF_INET, socket.SOCK_DGRAM)
s.bind(("", port))
print "waiting on port:", port
while 1:
    data, addr = s.recvfrom(1024)
    print data
```

Instead of having a listen() function, a UDP server has to open a socket and wait to receive incoming packets. As is evident from the code snippet, there is no listen() or accept() function. Save the above code and execute it from a terminal and then connect to it using the **NCAT** utility. NCAT is an alternative to Telnet, and it is more powerful than Telnet and packed with more features. Run the program and, in another terminal window, use NCAT. Here is the output of the execution of the program and NCAT:

```
pi@raspberrypi ~/book/chapter14 $ nc localhost 5000 -u -v
Connection to localhost 5000 port [udp/*] succeeded!

Hello
Ok
```

The -u flag in the command indicates the UDP protocol. The message we send should be displayed on the server terminal.

An echo server using Python UDP sockets

Here is the code for an echo server in Python:

```
import socket
import sys

HOST = ''   # Symbolic name meaning all available interfaces
PORT = 8888 # Arbitrary non-privileged port

# Datagram (udp) socket
try :
    s = socket.socket(socket.AF_INET, socket.SOCK_DGRAM)
    print 'Socket created'
except socket.error, msg :
    print 'Failed to create socket. Error Code : ' + str(msg[0]) + '
Message ' + msg[1]
    sys.exit()


# Bind socket to local host and port
try:
    s.bind((HOST, PORT))
except socket.error , msg:
    print 'Bind failed. Error Code : ' + str(msg[0]) + ' Message '
    + msg[1]
    sys.exit()

print 'Socket bind complete'

#now keep talking with the client
while 1:
    # receive data from client (data, addr)
    d = s.recvfrom(1024)
    data = d[0]
    addr = d[1]

    if not data:
        break

    reply = 'OK...' + data
```

```
        s.sendto(reply , addr)
        print 'Message[' + addr[0] + ':' + str(addr[1]) + '] - ' +
        data.strip()

    s.close()
```

This program will start a UDP server process on the mentioned port (in our case, it's 8888). Save the program and run it in a terminal. To test the program, open another terminal and use the NCAT utility to connect to this server, as follows:

```
pi@raspberrypi ~/book/chapter14 $ nc -vv localhost 8888 -u
Connection to localhost 8888 port [udp/*] succeeded!
OK...XOK...XOK...XOK...XOK...X
OK...
Hello
OK...Hello
How are you?
OK...How are you?
```

Use NCAT again to send messages to the UDP server, and the UDP server will reply back with OK... prefixed to the message.

The server process terminal also displays the details about the client connected, as follows:

```
$ python prog2.py
Socket created
Socket bind complete
Message[127.0.0.1:46622] - Hello
Message[127.0.0.1:46622] - How are you?
```

It is important to note that unlike a TCP server, a UDP server can handle multiple clients directly as there is no explicit connection with a client (hence connectionless). It can receive from any client and send a reply to it. No threads are required as we do in TCP servers.

A UDP client

The code for a UDP client is as follows:

```
import socket    #for sockets
import sys  #for exit
```

```
# create dgram udp socket
try:
    s = socket.socket(socket.AF_INET, socket.SOCK_DGRAM)
except socket.error:
    print 'Failed to create socket'
    sys.exit()

host = 'localhost';
port = 8888;

while(1) :
    msg = raw_input('Enter message to send : ')

    try :
        #Set the whole string
        s.sendto(msg, (host, port))

        # receive data from client (data, addr)
        d = s.recvfrom(1024)
        reply = d[0]
        addr = d[1]

        print 'Server reply : ' + reply

    except socket.error, msg:
        print 'Error Code : ' + str(msg[0]) + ' Message ' + msg[1]
        sys.exit()
```

The client will connect to the UDP server and exchange messages as follows:

```
pi@raspberrypi ~/book/chapter14 $ python prog3.py
Enter message to send : Hello
Server reply : OK...Hello
Enter message to send : How are you
Server reply : OK...How are you
Enter message to send : Ok
Server reply : OK...Ok
Enter message to send :
```

The programs for the UDP protocol are simple to code as there are no explicit connections from the UDP clients to the UDP server.

In the next subsection, we will learn about TCP sockets.

The architecture of TCP sockets

The following is a diagram of the TCP client-server architecture:

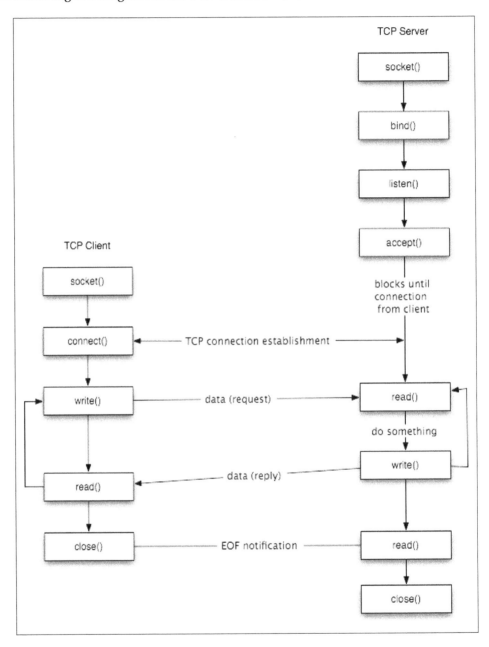

Creating a TCP socket

Here is an example of creating a TCP socket:

```
import socket    #for sockets

create an AF_INET, STREAM socket (TCP)
s = socket.socket(socket.AF_INET, socket.SOCK_STREAM)

print 'Socket Created'
```

The `socket.socket()` function creates a socket and returns a socket descriptor, which can be used in other socket-related functions.

This code will create a socket with the following properties:

- Address family: `AF_INET` (this is for IP version 4, or IPv4)
- Type: `SOCK_STREAM` (this specifies a connection-oriented protocol, that is, TCP)

If any of the socket functions fail, then Python throws an exception called `socket.error`, which must be caught as follows:

```
import socket    #for sockets
import sys   for exit

try:
    create an AF_INET, STREAM socket (TCP)
    s = socket.socket(socket.AF_INET, socket.SOCK_STREAM)
except socket.error, msg:
    print 'Failed to create socket. Error code: ' + str(msg[0]) + ' ,
Error message : ' + msg[1]
    sys.exit();

print 'Socket Created'
```

In this way, we have created a TCP socket successfully. We can connect to a server, for example, `https://www.google.com`, using this socket.

Connecting to a server with a TCP socket

We can connect to a remote server on a certain port number. We need two things for this: the IP address of the remote server we are connecting to and a port number to connect to. We will use the IP address of `https://www.google.com` as a sample in the following code.

First, we need to get the IP address of the remote host or URL, since before connecting to a remote host, its IP address is required. In Python, obtaining the IP address is quite simple:

```
import socket    #for sockets
import sys  #for exit

try:
    #create an AF_INET, STREAM socket (TCP)
    s = socket.socket(socket.AF_INET, socket.SOCK_STREAM)
except socket.error, msg:
    print 'Failed to create socket. Error code: ' + str(msg[0]) + ' ,
Error message : ' + msg[1]
    sys.exit();


print 'Socket Created'


host = 'www.google.com'

try:
    remote_ip = socket.gethostbyname( host )

except socket.gaierror:
    #could not resolve
    print 'Hostname could not be resolved. Exiting'
    sys.exit()

print 'Ip address of ' + host + ' is ' + remote_ip
```

Now that we have the IP address of the remote host or URL, we can connect to it on a certain port using the connect() function:

```
import socket    #for sockets
import sys  #for exit

try:
    create an AF_INET, STREAM socket (TCP)
    s = socket.socket(socket.AF_INET, socket.SOCK_STREAM)
except socket.error, msg:
    print 'Failed to create socket. Error code: ' + str(msg[0]) + ' ,
Error message : ' + msg[1]
    sys.exit();


print 'Socket Created'
```

```
host = 'www.google.com'
port = 80

try:
    remote_ip = socket.gethostbyname( host )

except socket.gaierror:
    could not resolve
    print 'Hostname could not be resolved. Exiting'
    sys.exit()

print 'Ip address of ' + host + ' is ' + remote_ip

Connect to remote server
s.connect((remote_ip , port))

print 'Socket Connected to ' + host + ' on ip ' + remote_ip
```

Run the program and notice that its output in the terminal is as follows:

pi@raspberrypi ~/book/chapter14 $ python prog4.py

Socket Created

Ip address of www.google.com is 74.125.236.83

Socket Connected to www.google.com on ip 74.125.236.83

It creates a TCP socket and then connects to a remote host. If we try connecting to a port different from port 80, then we should not be able to connect, which indicates that the port is not open for any connections. This logic can be used to build a port scanner.

> The concept of *connections* applies to SOCK_STREAM/TCP type of sockets. A connection means an explicit or reliable stream or pipeline of data such that there can be multiple such streams and each can have communication of its own. Think of this as a pipe that is not interfered with by data from other pipes. Another important property of stream connections is that the packets have an order or sequence; hence, they are always sent, arrive, and are processed in order.
>
> Other sockets, such as UDP, ICMP, and ARP, don't have the concept of an explicit *connection* or pipeline. These are connectionless communications, as we have seen with an example in the case of UDP. This means that we keep sending or receiving packets from anybody and everybody.

The `sendall()` function will send all the data. Let's send some data to https://www.google.com. The code for it is as follows:

```
import socket    #for sockets
import sys  #for exit

try:
    #create an AF_INET, STREAM socket (TCP)
    s = socket.socket(socket.AF_INET, socket.SOCK_STREAM)
except socket.error, msg:
    print 'Failed to create socket. Error code: ' + str(msg[0]) + ' ,
Error message : ' + msg[1]
    sys.exit();

print 'Socket Created'

host = 'www.google.com'
port = 80

try:
    remote_ip = socket.gethostbyname( host )

except socket.gaierror:
    #could not resolve
    print 'Hostname could not be resolved. Exiting'
    sys.exit()

print 'Ip address of ' + host + ' is ' + remote_ip

#Connect to remote server
s.connect((remote_ip , port))

print 'Socket Connected to ' + host + ' on ip ' + remote_ip

#Send some data to remote server
message = "GET / HTTP/1.1\r\n\r\n"

try :
    #Set the whole string
    s.sendall(message)
except socket.error:
    #Send failed
    print 'Send failed'
    sys.exit()

print 'Message send successfully'
```

In this example, we first connect to an IP address and then send the string message GET / HTTP/1.1\r\n\r\n to it. The message is actually an HTTP command to fetch the main page of the website.

Now that we have sent some data, it's time to receive a reply from the server. So let's do it.

Receiving data from the server

The recv() function is used to receive data on a socket. In the following example, we will send a message and receive a reply from the server with Python:

```
import socket   #for sockets
import sys  #for exit

#create an INET, STREAMing socket
try:
    s = socket.socket(socket.AF_INET, socket.SOCK_STREAM)
except socket.error:
    print 'Failed to create socket'
    sys.exit()

print 'Socket Created'

host = 'www.google.com';
port = 80;

try:
    remote_ip = socket.gethostbyname( host )

except socket.gaierror:
    #could not resolve
    print 'Hostname could not be resolved. Exiting'
    sys.exit()

#Connect to remote server
s.connect((remote_ip , port))

print 'Socket Connected to ' + host + ' on ip ' + remote_ip

#Send some data to remote server
message = "GET / HTTP/1.1\r\n\r\n"
```

```
try :
    #Set the whole string
    s.sendall(message)
except socket.error:
    #Send failed
    print 'Send failed'
    sys.exit()

print 'Message send successfully'

#Now receive data
reply = s.recv(4096)

print reply
```

Your web browser also does the same thing when you use it to open `www.google.com`.

This socket activity represents a client socket. A client is a system that connects to a remote host to fetch the required data.

The other type of socket activity is called a server system. A server is a system that uses sockets to receive incoming connections and provide them with the required data. It is just the opposite of the client system. So, `https://www.google.com` is a server system and a web browser is a client system. To be more specific, `https://www.google.com` is an HTTP server and a web browser is an HTTP client.

Programming socket servers

Now, we move on to learning how to program socket servers. Servers basically perform the following sequence of tasks:

1. Open a socket
2. Bind to an address (and port)
3. Listen for incoming client connection requests
4. Accept connections
5. Receive/send data from/to clients

We already know to open a socket. So, the next thing to learn will be how to bind it.

Binding a socket

The `bind()` function can be used to bind a socket to a particular IP address and port. It needs a `sockaddr_in` structure similar to the `connect()` function:

```
import socket
import sys

HOST = ''   # Symbolic name meaning all available interfaces
PORT = 8888 # Arbitrary non-privileged port

s = socket.socket(socket.AF_INET, socket.SOCK_STREAM)
print 'Socket created'

try:
    s.bind((HOST, PORT))
except socket.error , msg:
    print 'Bind failed. Error Code : ' + str(msg[0]) + ' Message ' +
msg[1]
    sys.exit()

print 'Socket bind complete'
```

Now that the binding is done, it's time to make the socket listen to incoming connection requests. We bind a socket to a particular IP address and a certain port number. By doing this, we ensure that all incoming data packets directed towards this port number are received by the server application.

Also, there cannot be more than one socket bound to the same port.

Listening for incoming connections

After binding a socket to a particular port, the next thing we need to do is listen for incoming connections. For this, we need to switch the socket to listening mode. The `socket_listen()` function is used to put the socket in listening mode. To accomplish this, we need to add the following line after the bind code:

```
s.listen(10)
print 'Socket now listening'
```

The parameter of the `listen()` function is called the **backlog**. It is used to control the number of incoming connections that are kept waiting if the program using that port is already busy. So, by mentioning `10`, we mean that if 10 connections are already waiting to be processed, then the eleventh new connection request shall be rejected. This will be clearer after checking `socket_accept()`.

Here is the code to do that:

```
import socket
import sys

HOST = ''    # Symbolic name meaning all available interfaces
PORT = 8888 # Arbitrary non-privileged port

s = socket.socket(socket.AF_INET, socket.SOCK_STREAM)
print 'Socket created'

try:
    s.bind((HOST, PORT))
except socket.error , msg:
    print 'Bind failed. Error Code : ' + str(msg[0]) + ' Message ' +
msg[1]
    sys.exit()

print 'Socket bind complete'

s.listen(10)
print 'Socket now listening'

#wait to accept a connection - blocking call
conn, addr = s.accept()

#display client information
print 'Connected with ' + addr[0] + ':' + str(addr[1])
```

Run the program. It should show you the following:

```
pi@raspberrypi ~/book/chapter14 $ python prog7.py
Socket created
Socket bind complete
Socket now listening
```

So now, this program is waiting for incoming client connections on port 8888. Don't close this program; ensure that you keep it running.

Now, a client can connect to the server on this port. We will use the Telnet client for testing this. Open a terminal and type this:

```
$ telnet localhost 8888
```

It will immediately show the following:

```
pi@raspberrypi ~/book/chapter14 $ telnet localhost 8888
Trying 127.0.0.1...
Connected to localhost.
Escape character is '^]'.
Connection closed by foreign host.
pi@raspberrypi ~/book/chapter14 $
```

And this is what the server will show:

```
pi@raspberrypi ~/book/chapter14 $ python prog7.py
Socket created
Socket bind complete
Socket now listening
Connected with 127.0.0.1:59954
```

So now, we can see that the client is connected to the server. We accepted an incoming connection but closed it immediately. There are lots of tasks that can be accomplished after an incoming connection is established. The connection was established between two hosts for the purpose of communication. So let's reply to the client.

The sendall() function can be used to send something to the socket of the incoming connection, and the client should be able to receive it. Here is the code for that:

```
import socket
import sys

HOST = ''    # Symbolic name meaning all available interfaces
PORT = 8888 # Arbitrary non-privileged port

s = socket.socket(socket.AF_INET, socket.SOCK_STREAM)
print 'Socket created'

try:
    s.bind((HOST, PORT))
except socket.error , msg:
    print 'Bind failed. Error Code : ' + str(msg[0]) + ' Message '
    + msg[1]
    sys.exit()

print 'Socket bind complete'
```

```
    s.listen(10)
    print 'Socket now listening'

    #wait to accept a connection - blocking call
    conn, addr = s.accept()

    print 'Connected with ' + addr[0] + ':' + str(addr[1])

    #now keep talking with the client
    data = conn.recv(1024)
    conn.sendall(data)

    conn.close()
    s.close()
```

Run this code in a terminal window and connect to this server using Telnet from another terminal; you should be able to see this:

pi@raspberrypi ~/book/chapter14 $ telnet localhost 8888

Trying 127.0.0.1...

Connected to localhost.

Escape character is '^]'.

happy

happy

Connection closed by foreign host.

So, the client (Telnet) received a reply from the server.

We can see that the connection is closed immediately after this, simply because the server program terminates immediately after accepting the request and responding with the reply. A server process is supposed to be running all the time; the simplest way to accomplish this is to iterate the `accept` method in a loop so that it can receive incoming connections all the time.

So, a live server will always be up and running. The code for this is as follows:

```
    import socket
    import sys

    HOST = ''   # Symbolic name meaning all available interfaces
    PORT = 5000 # Arbitrary non-privileged port

    s = socket.socket(socket.AF_INET, socket.SOCK_STREAM)
```

```
print 'Socket created'

try:
    s.bind((HOST, PORT))
except socket.error , msg:
    print 'Bind failed. Error Code : ' + str(msg[0]) + ' Message '
    + msg[1]
    sys.exit()

print 'Socket bind complete'

s.listen(10)
print 'Socket now listening'

#now keep talking with the client
while 1:
    #wait to accept a connection - blocking call
    conn, addr = s.accept()
    print 'Connected with ' + addr[0] + ':' + str(addr[1])

    data = conn.recv(1024)
    reply = 'OK...' + data
    if not data:
        break

    conn.sendall(reply)

conn.close()
s.close()
```

Now run this server program in a terminal, and open three other terminals.

From each of the three terminals, perform a Telnet to the server port.

Each of the Telnet terminals will show output as follows:

```
pi@raspberrypi ~/book/chapter14 $ telnet localhost 5000
Trying 127.0.0.1...
Connected to localhost.
Escape character is '^]'.
happy
OK .. happy
Connection closed by foreign host.
```

The server terminal will show the following:

```
pi@raspberrypi ~/book/chapter14 $ python prog9.py
Socket created
Socket bind complete
Socket now listening
Connected with 127.0.0.1:60225
Connected with 127.0.0.1:60237
Connected with 127.0.0.1:60239
```

So now, the server is up and the Telnet terminals are also connected to it. Now, terminate the server program. All Telnet terminals will show `Connection closed by foreign host`.

Handling multiple connections

To handle every connection, we need separate handling code to run along with the main server thread, which accepts incoming connection requests. One way to achieve this is to use threads. The main server program accepts an incoming connection request and provisions a new thread to handle communication for the connection, and then, the server goes back to accept more incoming connection requests.

This is the required code:

```python
import socket
import sys
from thread import *

HOST = ''   # Symbolic name meaning all available interfaces
PORT = 8888 # Arbitrary non-privileged port

s = socket.socket(socket.AF_INET, socket.SOCK_STREAM)
print 'Socket created'

#Bind socket to local host and port
try:
    s.bind((HOST, PORT))
except socket.error , msg:
    print 'Bind failed. Error Code : ' + str(msg[0]) + ' Message '
    + msg[1]
    sys.exit()

print 'Socket bind complete'
```

```
#Start listening on socket
s.listen(10)
print 'Socket now listening'

#Function for handling connections. This will be used to create
threads
def clientthread(conn):
    #Sending message to connected client
    conn.send('Welcome to the server. Type something and hit
    enter\n') #send only takes string

    #infinite loop so that function do not terminate and thread do
    not end.
    while True:

        #Receiving from client
        data = conn.recv(1024)
        reply = 'OK...' + data
        if not data:
            break

        conn.sendall(reply)

    #came out of loop
    conn.close()

#now keep talking with the client
while 1:
    #wait to accept a connection - blocking call
    conn, addr = s.accept()
    print 'Connected with ' + addr[0] + ':' + str(addr[1])

    #start new thread takes 1st argument as a function name to be
    run, second is the tuple of arguments to the function.
    start_new_thread(clientthread ,(conn,))

s.close()
```

Run this server code and open three terminals like before. Now, the server will create a thread for each client connecting to it.

The Telnet terminals will show output as follows:

```
pi@raspberrypi ~/book/chapter14 $ telnet localhost 8888
Trying 127.0.0.1...
Connected to localhost.
Escape character is '^]'.
Welcome to the server. Type something and hit enter
hi
OK...hi
asd
OK...asd
cv
OK...cv
```

The server terminal will look like this:

```
pi@raspberrypi ~/book/chapter14 $ python prog10.py
Socket created
Socket bind complete
Socket now listening
Connected with 127.0.0.1:60730
Connected with 127.0.0.1:60731
```

This connection handler takes the input from the client and replies with the same.

Looking back

By now, we have learned the basics of socket programming in Python. When testing these programs, if you face the following error, simply change the port number, and the server will run fine:

```
Bind failed. Error Code : 98 Message Address already in use
```

A Telnet client in Python

The Telnet client is a simple command-line program that is used to connect to socket servers and exchange messages. The following is an example of how to use Telnet to connect to `https://www.google.com` and fetch the homepage:

```
$ telnet www.google.com 80
```

This command will connect to www.google.com on port 80.

```
$ telnet www.google.com 80
Trying 74.125.236.69...
Connected to www.google.com.
Escape character is '^]'
```

Now that it is connected, the Telnet command can take user input and send it to the respective server, and whatever the server replies will be displayed in the terminal. For example, send the HTTP GET command in the following format and hit *Enter* twice:

```
GET / HTTP/1.1
```

Sending this will generate a response from the server. Now we will make a similar Telnet program. The program is simple: we will implement a program that takes user input and fetches results from the remote server in parallel using the threads. One thread will keep receiving messages from the server and another will keep taking in user input. But there is another way to do this apart from threads: the select() function. This function allows you to monitor multiple sockets or streams for readability and will generate an event if any of the sockets are ready.

The code for it is as follows:

```
import socket, select, string, sys

#main function
if __name__ == "__main__":

    if(len(sys.argv) < 3) :
        sys.exit()

    host = sys.argv[1]
    port = int(sys.argv[2])

    s = socket.socket(socket.AF_INET, socket.SOCK_STREAM)
    s.settimeout(2)

    # connect to remote host
    try :
        s.connect((host, port))
    except :
        print 'Unable to connect'
        sys.exit()
```

```
      print 'Connected to remote host'

while 1:
    socket_list = [sys.stdin, s]

    # Get the list sockets which are readable
    read_sockets, write_sockets, error_sockets =
    select.select(socket_list , [], [])

    for sock in read_sockets:
        #incoming message from remote server
        if sock == s:
            data = sock.recv(4096)
            if not data :
                print 'Connection closed'
                sys.exit()
            else :
                #print data
                sys.stdout.write(data)

        #user entered a message
        else :
            msg = sys.stdin.readline()
            s.send(msg)
```

The execution of this program is shown here. It connects to the remote host `google.com`.

```
$ python telnet.py google.com 80
Connected to remote host
```

Once connected, it shows the appropriate connected message. Once the message is displayed, type in some message to send to the remote server. Type the same GET message and send it by hitting *Enter* twice. A response will be generated.

A chat program

In the previous section, we went through the basics of creating a socket server and client in Python. In this section, we will write a chat application in Python that is powered by Python sockets.

The chat application we are going to make will be a common chat room rather than a peer-to-peer chat. So this means that multiple chat users can connect to the chat server and exchange messages. Every message is broadcast to every connected chat user.

The chat server

The chat server performs the following tasks:

- It accepts multiple incoming connections for the client.

- It reads incoming messages from each client and broadcasts them to all the other connected clients.

The following is the code for the chat server:

```
import socket, select

#Function to broadcast chat messages to all connected clients
def broadcast_data (sock, message):
    #Do not send the message to master socket and the client who
    has send us the message
    for socket in CONNECTION_LIST:
        if socket != server_socket and socket != sock :
            try :
                socket.send(message)
            except :
                # broken socket connection may be, chat client
                pressed ctrl+c for example
                socket.close()
                CONNECTION_LIST.remove(socket)

if __name__ == "__main__":

    # List to keep track of socket descriptors
    CONNECTION_LIST = []
    RECV_BUFFER = 4096 # Advisable to keep it as an exponent of 2
    PORT = 5000

    server_socket = socket.socket(socket.AF_INET,
    socket.SOCK_STREAM)
    # this has no effect, why ?
    server_socket.setsockopt(socket.SOL_SOCKET,
    socket.SO_REUSEADDR, 1)
    server_socket.bind(("0.0.0.0", PORT))
    server_socket.listen(10)

    # Add server socket to the list of readable connections
    CONNECTION_LIST.append(server_socket)

    print "Chat server started on port " + str(PORT)
```

```
        while 1:
            # Get the list sockets which are ready to be read through
    select
            read_sockets,write_sockets,error_sockets =
            select.select(CONNECTION_LIST,[],[])

            for sock in read_sockets:
                #New connection
                if sock == server_socket:
                    # Handle the case in which there is a new
                    connection recieved through server_socket
                    sockfd, addr = server_socket.accept()
                    CONNECTION_LIST.append(sockfd)
                    print "Client (%s, %s) connected" % addr

                    broadcast_data(sockfd, "[%s:%s] entered room\n" %
                    addr)

                #Some incoming message from a client
                else:
                    # Data received from client, process it
                    try:
                        #In Windows, sometimes when a TCP program
                        closes abruptly,
                        # a "Connection reset by peer" exception will
                        be thrown
                        data = sock.recv(RECV_BUFFER)
                        if data:
                            broadcast_data(sock, "\r" + '<' +
                            str(sock.getpeername()) + '> ' + data)

                    except:
                        broadcast_data(sock, "Client (%s, %s) is
                        offline" % addr)
                        print "Client (%s, %s) is offline" % addr
                        sock.close()
                        CONNECTION_LIST.remove(sock)
                        continue

    server_socket.close()
```

In this code, the server program opens up port 5000 to listen for incoming connections from the clients. The chat client must connect to the same port. We can change the port number if we want by specifying another number that is not used by any other program or process.

The server handles multiple chat clients with multiplexing based on the `select()` function. The `select()` function monitors all the client sockets and the master socket for any readable activity. If any of the client sockets are readable, then it means that one of the chat clients has sent a message to the server.

When the `select()` function returns, `read_sockets` will be an array consisting of all socket descriptors that are readable. When the master socket is readable, the server will accept the new connection. If any of the client sockets is readable, the server will read the message and broadcast it back to all the other clients except the one who sent the message. If the broadcast function fails to send the message to any of the clients, the client is presumed to be disconnected, the connection is closed, and the corresponding socket is removed from the connections list.

The chat client

Now, let's code the chat client that will connect to the chat server and exchange the messages. The chat client is based on the Telnet program in Python, which we have already worked on. It connects to a remote server and exchanges messages.

The chat client performs the following tasks:

- It listens for incoming messages from the server.
- It checks for user input, in case the user types in a message and then sends it to the chat server to which it is connected.

The client has to actually listen for server messages and user input simultaneously. To accomplish this, we can use the `select()` function. The `select()` function can monitor multiple sockets or file descriptors simultaneously for activity. When a message from the server arrives on the connected socket, it is readable, and when the user types a message from the keyboard and hits *Enter*, the `stdin` stream is readable.

So, the `select()` function has to monitor two streams: the first is the socket that is connected to the remote web server, and the second is `stdin` or terminal input stream from the keyboard. The `select()` function waits until some activity happens. So, after calling the `select()` function, the function itself will return only when either the server socket receives a message or the user enters a message using the keyboard. If nothing happens, it keeps on waiting.

We can create an array of the `stdin` file descriptor that is available from the `sys` module and the server sockets. Then, we call the `select()` function, passing it the list. The `select()` function returns a list of arrays that are readable, writable, or have an error.

Here is the Python code that implements the previous logic using the `select()` function as follows:

```python
import socket, select, string, sys

def prompt() :
    sys.stdout.write('<You> ')
    sys.stdout.flush()

#main function
if __name__ == "__main__":

    if(len(sys.argv) < 3) :
        print 'Usage : python telnet.py hostname port'
        sys.exit()

    host = sys.argv[1]
    port = int(sys.argv[2])

    s = socket.socket(socket.AF_INET, socket.SOCK_STREAM)
    s.settimeout(2)

    # connect to remote host
    try :
        s.connect((host, port))
    except :
        print 'Unable to connect'
        sys.exit()

    print 'Connected to remote host. Start sending messages'
    prompt()

    while 1:
        socket_list = [sys.stdin, s]

        # Get the list sockets which are readable
        read_sockets, write_sockets, error_sockets =
        select.select(socket_list , [], [])

        for sock in read_sockets:
            #incoming message from remote server
            if sock == s:
                data = sock.recv(4096)

                if not data :
                    print '\nDisconnected from chat server'
                    sys.exit()
                else :
                    #print data
                    sys.stdout.write(data)
```

```
                prompt()

        #user entered a message
        else :
            msg = sys.stdin.readline()
            s.send(msg)
            prompt()
```

Execute the chat client from multiple consoles as follows:

```
$ python telnet.py localhost 5000
Connected to remote host. Start sending messages
<You> hello
<You> I am fine
<('127.0.0.1', 38378)> ok good
<You>
on another console
<You> [127.0.0.1:39339] entered room
<('127.0.0.1', 39339)> hello
<('127.0.0.1', 39339)> I am fine
<You> ok good
```

In this way, the messages sent by one client can be seen on the terminal of the other client.

References

The code and definitions in this chapter have been referred to from a few online sources, as follows:

- http://www.binarytides.com/python-socket-programming-tutorial
- http://www.binarytides.com/python-socket-server-code-example
- http://www.binarytides.com/code-chat-application-server-client-sockets-python
- http://www.binarytides.com/code-telnet-client-sockets-python
- http://www.binarytides.com/programming-udp-sockets-in-python
- http://www.binarytides.com/socket-programming-c-linux-tutorial/
- http://www.diffen.com/difference/TCP_vs_UDP
- http://eprints.uthm.edu.my/7531/1/FAYAD_MOHAMMED_MOHAMMED_GHAWBAR_24.pdf
- http://www.cs.dartmouth.edu/~campbell/cs60/UDPsockets.jpg
- http://www.cs.dartmouth.edu/~campbell/cs60/TCPsockets.jpg

Exercise

Additionally, you can learn more about raw sockets in Python from the following links:

- `http://www.binarytides.com/raw-socket-programming-in-python-linux`
- `http://www.binarytides.com/python-syn-flood-program-raw-sockets-linux`

Summary

In this chapter, we learned about the concepts required to understand the transfer of data between two or more machines, in which the sender is termed as a server and the receiver is termed as the client. We also learned the basics of establishing a connection between a server and a client.

We built both UDP and TCP socket programs using Python and learned how to perform tasks such as connecting to a server, sending messages, receiving messages, and so on. Finally, we combined all that we learned to create a simple chat program that would allow two users to communicate with each other. We can now build our own instant messaging service!

Now that we are at the end of the book, take some time to go over the projects that you have successfully built. We have completed some projects, ranging from the beginner level to the advanced level, and learned a lot about the intricacies of working with the Raspberry Pi and all its parallel concepts firsthand. Starting from the introduction of the Raspberry Pi to projects such as motion detection from images and intruder detection using the concepts of the Internet of Things, we have covered almost everything that you would require to build some interesting projects of your own.

We hope this inspires you to keep on building fun projects that are not only interesting to set up and cool to watch but also useful to the world in general. Keep on hacking!

Newer Raspberry Pi Models

The latest additions in the Raspberry Pi family are the Raspberry Pi Zero and Raspberry Pi 3. We did not discuss these new additions in the earlier chapters. So, let's focus on a few details of both these new members of the Raspberry Pi family.

The Raspberry Pi Zero

The size of a Raspberry Pi Zero is half the size of a Model A+. This is ideal for embedded projects where size and power requirements are stringent. Here are the specifications for the Raspberry Pi Zero:

- A 1-GHz, single-core CPU
- 512 MB of RAM
- Mini HDMI and USB on-the-go ports
- Micro USB power
- A HAT-compatible 40-pin header
- Composite video and reset headers

Here is an image of the Pi Zero, obtained from www.wired.co.uk:

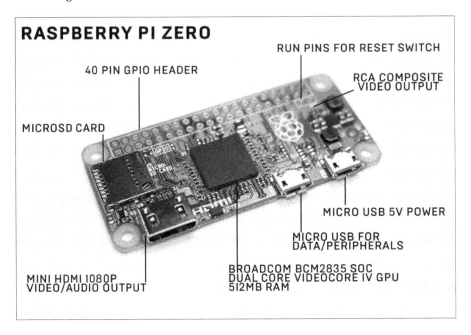

There are two ways in which we can connect the Pi Zero to a display:

- Using mini-HDMI-to-HDMI converter, shown here:

You can purchase one from Adafruit, using these links:
https://www.adafruit.com/products/2775
https://www.adafruit.com/products/2819

* Also, we can use VGA for display. For this, we need to use a mini-HDMI-to-VGA adapter.

 This can be purchased at
https://www.adafruit.com/products/3048.

For conveniently using the GPIO pins of the Pi Zero, you can use any one of the following two-pin strip GPIO headers:

- `https://www.adafruit.com/products/2822`

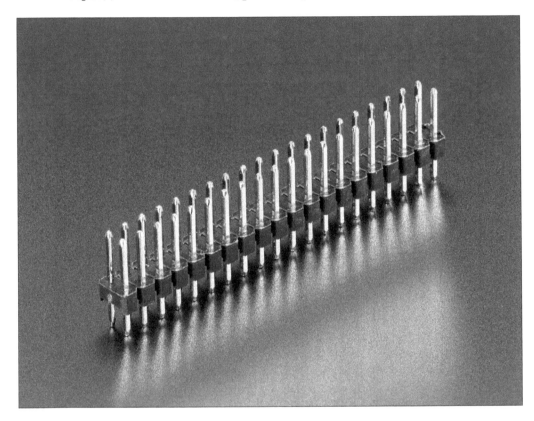

- https://www.adafruit.com/products/2823

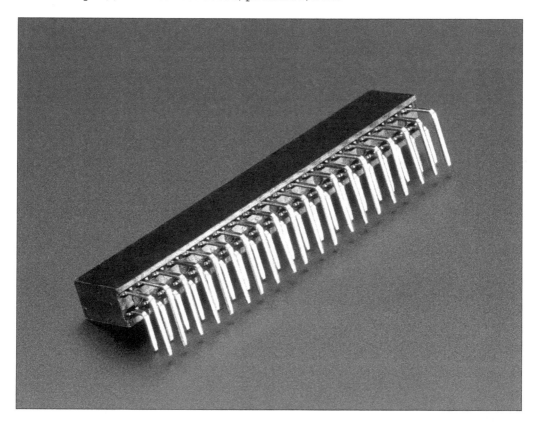

Also, for connecting various devices, a mini-USB-to-USB converter can be used.

This can be obtained from `https://www.adafruit.com/products/2910`.

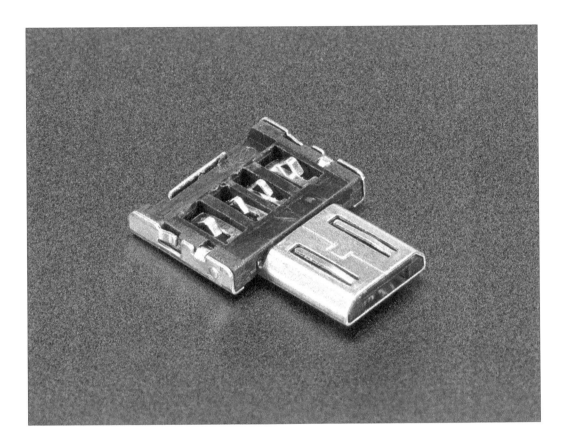

The Raspberry Pi 3

The Raspberry Pi 3 is the latest addition to the Raspberry Pi family. It is a third-generation Raspberry Pi. It replaced the Raspberry Pi 2 Model B in February 2016. Compared to the Pi 2, it has the following features:

- A 1.2-GHz 64-bit quad-core ARMv8 CPU
- 802.11n onboard wireless LAN
- Bluetooth 4.1
- **Bluetooth Low Energy (BLE)**

Also, like the Raspberry Pi 2, also has the following features:

- Four USB ports
- 40 GPIO pins
- A full-HDMI port
- An Ethernet port
- A combined 3.5mm audio jack and composite video
- A camera interface (CSI)
- A display interface (DSI)
- A micro-SD card slot (now push-pull rather than push-push)
- A VideoCore IV 3D graphics core

The form factor of the Pi 3 is identical to that of the Pi 2 and Pi 1 Model B+. The Pi 3 has complete backward compatibility with the Pi 1 and 2.

The product description for the Pi Zero and Pi 3 can be found on Raspberry Pi's official product pages:

https://www.raspberrypi.org/products/pi-zero/

https://www.raspberrypi.org/products/raspberry-pi-3-model-b/

Index

G

GalaxSee
  about 195
  installing 196-199
  URL 196
GalaxSee program
  executing 199
GPIO (general purpose input/output) 73
GPIO pins
  defining 74-76
GPU (Graphics Processor Unit) 17
GrovePi
  defining 147-149
  setting up 149-153
  URL 149
GrovePi+
  URL 149

H

humidity and temperature sensor
  URL 148
  using 154-156

I

image color channels
  image, negating 123
  merging 122, 123
  splitting 122, 123
image properties
  retrieving 117
images
  arithmetic operations 118-122
  logical operations 124, 125
  matplotlib, using 112-114
  thresholding 131-133
  working with 109-112
Internet of Things
  defining 162
Internet Protocol (IP) 232
Intruder detection system 157, 158
Itseez
  URL 102

L

Last In First Out (LIFO) 51
LED
  URL 148
LED Blinker
  building 76-78
  button, connecting 78, 79
Linux
  reference 13
logic operators
  used, in Python 87

M

Mac OS
  reference 13
matplotlib
  URL 114
Minecraft
  URL 29
Minecraft Pi
  Action control 35-37
  defining 29
  Movement control 34, 35
  other controls, defining 38
  playing 30-33
  Python programming, used for 38-44
  URL 32
Minecraft Pi Python API
  URL 44
MMD-1 (Mini Micro Designer 1) 2
morphological transformations
  used, on images 141, 142
motion detection 142-145
MPI4PY
  configuring 180-184
  installing 180-188
mpi4py library
  URL 188
MPICH2
  configuring 180-184
  installing 180-184
MPICH library
  installing 184, 185
  URL 184

www.ingramcontent.com/pod-product-compliance
Lightning Source LLC
Chambersburg PA
CBHW060519060326
40690CB00017B/3328